Whispers from the Soul

Whispers from the Soul

E. Milton Scott

VANTAGE PRESS
New York

Published by Vantage Press, Inc.
516 West 34th Street, New York, New York 10001

Manufactured in the United States of America
ISBN: 0-533-14392-6

Library of Congress Catalog Card No.: 2002093344

0 9 8 7 6 5 4 3 2 1

To
Martha and Beth

Contents

Part II: A King's Elegance

Part III: More Than Now

Introduction

Musing

To acknowledge that selections or groupings of poems have taken three, five, or ten years to write may disclose the terminal time, but each poem scrapes out a space from a lifetime. How far back or forward one may go to reach or miss the present moment of a creative synapse must remain undetectable. Suffice it to write, poetry is released when the spirit moves the soul's recognition.

These chosen words herein, as I believe is the case with all literature, are valuable in the ways the language enhances minds intellectually and emotionally. The aim has been to achieve some measure of understanding and discovery between myself and the reader. The words are attempts to communicate thoughts and feelings on reflections of the truth.

Once I was asked, "What are your poems about?" My answer was, "My poems are about persons, animals, and things." Probably not understood by the questioner, I meant persons are those who feel, make choices, and are unique. Animals, although inferior to persons, are living creatures I think about, admire, respect, and whom, I imagine, like everyone, tend to see as human reflectors. Things are circumstances, events both true and imagined, as well as entities, ideas, and actions.

While it would be unusual for one to find all poems to one's interest or liking, they all became valuable to me because they helped me realize my choices, my selections for contact—to find communicable ways to suggest some empathy with and for. In short, meanings are found within each person as he/she sees the world. Fortunately or unfortunately, final judgment lies with the readers, who interpret, think about, and determine the poem's worth to themselves. Written years ago, the "Polemical Introduction" to *Anatomy of Criticism* by Northrop Frye (1957) included a statement about critics being the final judges of the value of a poem's meaning: "The reason for this is an inability to distinguish literature from the descriptive or assertive writing which derives from the active will and conscious mind, and which is primarily concerned to 'say' something."

Soft rushing nuances or shades of meaning have eased me into writing delicate thoughts as they played with my consciousness. I've mused about them in images and ideas that drew my focus so that they gathered strength and became significant to me. As Thomas Moore wrote in *Care of the Soul,* "The Soul and Power," 1992, "The power of the soul . . . is more like a great reservoir or, in transitory imagery, like a force of water in a fast rushing river." Entertaining transitory mental impressions I concentrated on writing about them in poetic forms before they could escape into my daily existence.

To those who would find a presence in these imaginings, effects of words and sounds, the tensive binds of words, perhaps one could assume more than a decorous sense and reach into the poems. To those I offer the following:

To Become the Poem

As one may understand it to be,
the reader bends over it to see;
like a bird pecks at what is below
and will take it in or let it go.
If sustenance can't be found in words,
the pecking is done, as will birds
perfunctorily pluck and nibble
to strike or find content, or quibble
and evade the words, or stroke a kiss,
touching a phrase one will not dismiss;
then the heart or mind will take a taste
and no longer shy away in haste;
then the heart will be enticed to feel
that a look, a smile, or sense is real;
then lines, phrases, or a verse return
with a presence drawing one's discern.

Whispers from the Soul

I

CENTER OF THINGS

The greatest need in the world at this moment is the transformation of human nature.

—Billy Graham, August 1997

Engaged for What Reason

Inside, so quiet, to breathe is an audible sound.
Outside, so frantic, are lively sounds so chirpy—
A bird, perhaps two, flying around over the ground.
Engaged for what reason but to know perky
In movements gives out the not uncommon hint
That spring is signaled by birds talking.
Talking or singing, who knows what is meant?
When such activity for many is just squawking,
Were it not that frightened flapping ducks do this
Loudly or harshly, unlike birds, we may not miss
Lively and cheerful sounds and know birds do this.

From a distance who can tell if two have a wrangle?
So far away are we to know that we cannot hear.
Only when gestures appear there may be some angle
We think they have to differ, but we are not clear.
Yet compare them to seem humanlike we guess we know.
We, the most complex species on the earth,
Think because we can so easily watch the flow
And imagine beyond our knowledge only a dearth
Of information so minuscule we cannot know.

The human mind is quite complex for us to obtain
What is being thought at any given moment;
To wonder is so appealing for all of us to gain
Exact feelings and thoughts from another to foment
Some dispute we unwittingly construct from our own life—
Within ourselves depicting a scene reflecting our own strife,
That it must be true concerning a quite different life.

The turning, dipping and darting bird with a shrill sound
Is intermittently singing or chirping while flying around.
I cannot tell from hearing all the spring sweetness said
Just what is meant from moving beak and nodding head.

3

Churnings

Space years above do not change for me.
Seabed to surface rolls remain free.
They lather whatever shores in their touch
With a foam from ten thousands as much
As the winds and currents are driven
And change in swirls and eddies given
To lengths of vastness they move to be.
Days and nights of churnings on a spree
Take so many different fans of wind
That blow across and into no end.
Sometimes my face is calm and smooth
To await the urgings deepened grooves
Made from canyons below in depths
That surge and belch into countless steps:
My stomach gyrates an upward bounce,
Which in time does trench and denounce
The drifting calm resting below the air;
Then a retch to the surface up there,
Up where the free space of time does lie.
And again the wind's push from the sky
Carries me along to another place.
But all to rush and lift me through space
Settling again in water's terrain.

Into space rising to thwart disdain,
Seeking the freshness of somewhere else,
My calmness to storm does not erase
The inward struggle to outer face.
Seeing the sky, a hypnotic trance,
Does pull me up to find if by chance,
If it will release my soul to go
Away from the strain that moves so slow.
So much larger this ocean of doubt
Gives this length of space to reach far out
To a search through time to seek my heart,
To seek to move through new fields of light,
To see always and forever long sight.

Each day's rolls and surges come again
To reach as far as the inland's end.
Shores must wait on the water's lash edge
To hold against its smashing each ledge
To keep its limits invade out farther.

My search goes beyond each try to smother
Ups and down of turbulent sameness,
The torment of disguising inaneness.
At night the stars reach me in splendor.
Their grandiose touch from the Sender
Reaches to sparkle and shine my soul.
Love's longing no matter how each roll
Can want to climb the sky from its peak,
It does regard clear space's act of love.
Though limits are made for what must be,
Search goes on for image and destiny.

Statements of Attention

We are all so different, yet so alike;
Any wonder how we can relate to each other?
We make assumptions and think we can requite
Another's love without exploring any further.

So many philosophers discuss a being.
They provide us with surveys of why, we think,
That meaning can be found in mentally seeing
The reasons and results of thoughts they shrink
Until a telling statement will put us on the brink
Of where we might be if we could only know
Where something started and continued to grow
Through all of life with steady persistence,
Even when various pursuits tamper with our existence.

The wise have great powers of reflection.
Each pitfall they surmise with analytical inspection;
And then, out of it all
Comes a statement that somewhere may fall
On penetrable ears to minds for discovery
Of the path to take for eventual recovery.
But recover from what, asks the inscrutable cynic,
Who seems to be everywhere no matter the place,
To ask a question, initiating some clinic
To enlarge the content of knowledgeable space—
Some conundrum is posed maybe to amuse,
But more often to explain may irreparably confuse.

Such are those with whom we may pay attention,
With statements to explore or merely to mention,
But the relationships we somehow develop
Seem to continue and, thank God, envelop
Us for the good to gain from each unique invention.

A Turbulence

The other day overheard two kids talking
(Arguing would be more to the direction).
One had made a promise and now was balking.
Striking could be less to the selection—
New enemies might grow from the defection
Of one's allegiance now rising as a possibility.
The point seemed to have grown over insensibility.

A small two-person war could develop.
Could perceive a microcosm of something bigger;
Although the reason causes the feelings to envelop
The two with an argument increasing the chance to trigger
Some thoughtless violence to charge the situation,
Bringing about a poisoned separation,
Which demeans the friendship that should be nourished.
A growth impairs a closeness now pressing what once
    flourished.

The sky was closed away this morning.
Looked back out to a gray overcast that suddenly appeared.
How fast it came with such a forlorning
Cover that before, my glance never feared!
Will it grow even darker during the day?
From the overcast day come a blinding rain,
A part of living a turbulence that could hide a relational gain.

Looks Promising

"It looks promising," we sometimes say to someone.
Do we sometimes find ourselves saying it lightly to someone?
Can this phrase be taken by someone as a sign of hope?
Or does it draw a conclusion with little scope?

In the early morning when the sun begins to rise,
With the day dawning and it looks clear in the skies,
Depending on what one wants or wishes to take place,
A good phrase can give a relationship a budding grace.

It would be sad to say if most replies did not mean
Other than only some simple disinterested screen.
One may need the hope that the coming day will go well.
It's all anyone may need in such a test to make a friendship
    gel.

Does there have to be always some specific thought
For what is best to assure that comfort is sought?
It's something to think about when one is confronted.
"Looks promising" is better than being wittingly blunted.

Social Dilemma

The longing does often exist to explore a new dwelling,
A new abode to refresh the spirit and touch the soul.
Why do these searches continue the swelling
Of an understanding view that seems so compelling?
Is not the old satisfying and within one's control?
But it portends some mystery is growing there.
Even though the heart may be sublime with what we know,
We still seek that someplace destination to go where
The underscribed self is challenged to learn and grow.
The trouble is a plan may be needed for departure.
Does that mean there is too much baggage to carry,
Causing the traveler time to stop and unwittingly tarry?
Would seem like the plight of the arrowless archer,
Wanting to fling a marker at some distant place,
But must secure more certainty before the bow is bent—
A dilemma the seeker would most willingly erase.
On one hand, the target to reach and rush for intent;
On the other too much to take for fear—so hide
From others to be there to where the social collide
And mar the exploration because feelings are confused
With the original purpose somehow internally diffused.

Crease of Life

Walk out and feel it close around you.
So sudden it clasps and restricts the view.
As if the air comes pure and dense,
Like a sense in water to stretch and rinse,
The ingredient light has gone astray.
The indulgent fright is a prone delay
Between the day and eve that's past—
A blank of time stealth comes rubbing passed
When the body sinks into a loss of way.
When the mind breaches from a need to weigh
The prospects to find a place to go,
Where there's need to see and a space to grow.
The known to the unknown are not so clear
That the place to be will relieve the fear.
Though human minds created some paths
To reach out through less clear contrasts.
For every day there are the nights
We plod the times and miss the sights.
The light was made to open and whirl,
But must come parts where night must furl
Between the two, the day and night,
Comes hope to study, relieve the plight,
Brings time to think and time to ponder—
The crease of life to find and wonder.

The Between Place

Just to be walking through the gentle mist—
Just to be feeling what the facile air
Can be on the skin, the face, seems to be only a gist
For those who, if walking, want it to be always fair.
For we who want only a moisture trace
Of rain to notice just the lingering between place.

Is it the need to be exposed everywhere
That draws the heart and body into this space?
Though protective clothing is used anywhere.
The outer self is exposed to a vulnerable place.
Human resistance can test itself in the damp
Atmosphere of tender moments to trod and tramp.

Not so much is the moisture in a measured sense
A way to explore the dense and particled fall,
As it is a freshened exposure against that fence
That keeps us oftentimes from the call
Of natural existence to walk in the fine rain—
A walk of awakened love so hesitant and soft again.

After the caressing feel of the invisible drops,
And having paid attention to their loving touch,
Emotional inscription can do away with word props
To find in our felt lives not anymore so much
But the adventures in softness we often avoid,
And find wonderful times to be not annoyed.

Worth of a Moment Gone

The day begins with a whisper of light.
Something new is there to bless the air—
A promise of a new glow for a freshened sight
To create anew a start with nature's flair,
An attitude to bring to all a symbol of care.

An equal time is to see the waning day
To feel the joy of a fullness gone by—
The settling thoughts of a time to fade away.
When a collected moment, more than a sigh
Has come and gone, a time drawn nigh.

But what is the worth of a moment come
And the receding value of a moment gone?
To look ahead and back is only for some
The new and the old for an end to be shown
On a brief to be placed in one mind alone.

How can one find the truth of a moment past,
A bounded time so important in the scheme
Of all that is done in a life that is cast—
In the flow of motion found in the stream,
Which has come but the essence of a dream?

I sat on the bank and saw the water flow.
I saw in the water not still for me to know
Why it keeps going, continuing to move along.
When gone away from its momentary song,
Could I think back and feel my sight again,
And know the wonder of the beauty that had been?

On One Planet

Who is my neighbor? Let me see . . .
How near must I be to notice?
May I choose whom he will be?
Is it something to do deliberately?
Am I bringing up something considerately?

What is the reason? Look at you . . .
Stand there, ask me, such a question!
But to choose, must be some clue.
Was said today, at the club meeting,
Everyone living now has my greeting.

Live on one planet! Do you think . . .
This earth has but one life span.
Have the sense to avoid the brink.
If said later, we won't be here.
We help each other now, or no career.

All are our neighbor! You must believe.
Make it last as long as it can!
Choose all, ask all, work the reprieve.
It is something we do humanely.
In our giving we operate sanely.

Shadows of Life

Within the tonal wonders of the human mind,
Which ignite the power for each of us to detect,
We search only what fancy will take us to find.
From the sensing shadows indirection may reflect
Images from the words exchanged give us to see.
Mysteries appear from these sliding shadows of life.
And transitory meanings are less optioned to flee
When they are sensed without the transverse fife.
A silent solitude comes as a clear-voiced lyric
Into the spiritual strength of sight and size,
That otherwise thought to need a stressed pyrrhic—
Though not needed to engage an emotional rise.
What holds us in our prison that limits us to see
Outside the confines of, but for a reflective world,
Is the darkened figure in its infinite complexity.
Our inner workings make us long for details unfurled.

Ideal

They come to be with friends.
A group collects; another ends.
A sameness is there again.
A place to be together when.
Look to see who is there.
Those to find who will care,
Someone to say, eyes meet.
Enter and find warmth to greet,
A homing place all can feel
The search to have an ideal
To serve with each part
Of life to give a start.
Where worlds of good are done,
When talk with each is fun.
Sit and listen, time to share
How much life each can spare.
To look ahead, find the joy
How to give, how to employ
Truth to give what is fair;
And live a life to share.
Within walls a certain place,
All can find a certain grace.
Today all come and find
The goal to have a kind
Of use to put oneself
On a path off the shelf.
Free the spirit and soul's demand
That peace can be to understand.

Bereft of a Reply

Subtle breaks can be made for slightful pain.
Brutal rakes may be seen as an eddy gain.
Slants can be made through nauseous laughter—
From a moment's boast to a thud thereafter.
To settle stakes, a clown tries to steal
The calm will of one to take and feel
Without resource to come back, bereft of reply—
Must pause and think and miss a try
To fly up some wit not there for now—
A less practiced being, not prone to know how.
Where are those who free other's gears,
And use their minds to reduce other's fears—
Releasing the calm will of a shy and gentle soul,
And loosening the spiritual calm for their control?

Will to Discover

The borders in life are many by human design.
Strength in oneself is found in the tests
That each with diligence can find and not resign
From the journeys leading up to the rests
Among the trials that can lead to the brink.
There where all who travel must have the will to think.

The times to discover are open to all.
How can one know but to seek the edge
Of each encounter with care not to fall?
Hours that allow each experience comes a pledge
To search how far no matter the trail.
But the trail no matter, self must prevail.

Why seek the line that makes separation?
Why question the boundary that always exists?
To go too far will exceed the preparation,
Some will say, overextension leads to risks;
But how else to know what matters beyond,
If one only abides and does not respond.

The path must start with a study of the known.
Times one does not know from whence he came—
Chances are provided but often have let flown.
Each day's survival tempts one to do the same,
But where is the courage to try a different way—
To know that to learn is not found by delay.

The road to be taken summons one's courage—
The quality of spirit that lingers but enables
Must be there alone without others to encourage.
It is fear that holds one back and disables.
The heart and soul must not be found wanting—
Progress cannot be found if life is too daunting.

The Gift of Devotion

A gift is given when time is spent to teach,
Often thought that a mind must be sent to reach
Into whatever is beyond the current status bound,
But what is taught so often is close to the ground;
That is, what is known to be already found.
True that life to life here and now is first to see,
And the ethic of living must rule for all to be;
But to feed the soul reach is more than to agree.

Answers placed when the young begin to observe
Are given within what is often taught to preserve—
The sense of what is kind and fair for life.
The greater gift fills the spirit when want is rife
With desire to search further than a static notion
Of what today will give in monetarily upward motion.
The time to spend more needed for youthful urge
May be to entice the mind from some meandering splurge,
To zealously seek the unknown with uncompromising devotion.

Present for Us to Know

The beauty of a season can help us to detect
Where the spirit commands a sensory effect
Of all the growth and the given works that nourish
And present to us how life does flourish.

To rise in the morning light that strips the dew
From the bush beginning to bloom when night is through,
Rekindles the spirit's mediation of body and soul.
Life is evidenced anew from its flowering role.

The glorious color from reflected light to the eyes
Becomes clearer as it blazons down from the skies.
One must spend a little time to give pause and look.
The measured essence will be worth the time it took.

Indeed, no better way from view can be found
Than to reap the glistened rays from above to ground,
From which the enlivened things can touch the mind,
That after all is what rushes a soul to find.

Between

There where the space is between the earth and sky—
Something is there that can be seen and attended to.
Two points can help for a discovery that may defy.
When no reference is used to identify what is true,
The meaning to two is never there fixed for both,
Unless their minds will search for new mental growth.

Persons may reach out should they want to know
What the other thinks about some circumstance;
But how would one find that desire to grow
When one's own mind searches only from happenstance?
A unique mental or visual impact seems so clear—
The ordinary is less noticed within a usual atmosphere.

Relationships become a problem when two cannot feel
With the same intentional degree as the other.
But to relate is much more than the seal
Two think each one has, so seek not further.
The space where one locates what the other believes
Becomes unimportant regardless of what the other conceives.

We do not see to know but our own private thoughts.
We think we see persons just as they are.
It is only what is between rather than our valued oughts
That cause us to stop and seek not so far
As to discover what they see and let them find
The ways to be secure in parts of a single mind.

Words

We use them as our main form of expression—
A speech utterance intended to make some impression.
So much value is placed on their plentiful use,
So many ways that provide us with a means to induce.
Something is said, who knows if it has been read,
Often thought a medium for others to be led.
Words can be as assurance to someone in need,
But they can be misapplied to our sufferance of greed,
Which causes us to ask why are we listening
To this frontal example of some user's glistening.
May we have a true report, some tidings of information,
Rather than just retort, some speaking for one's inflation.
Often there is need to assert, affirm, and repair,
Not just one's pithy or sententious saying to spare.
One worthy can order, bid, request or demand:
But how often occur the words of misgotten command?
Oh, give us words that are backed by one's veracity,
Words that represent one's learned capacity,
Words from the mind and the human feeling heart
That help us to know their intended love from the start.
There is often a flooding of common and poisonous rumor
That does no good but makes anxious the consumer.
Give us all who can celebrate others with a phrase,
And reward ourselves for word-thoughts of care,
And produce from our minds an ensuing prayer
That our words will comfort and work to heal
Those who may struggle within the commonweal.

Her Whisper

She was tall, plump with a benign face.
Her red hair and double chin embraced a soft,
gentle countenance that emitted friendly
but serious looks that greeted each place
where she was with students, especially those
who had the good fortune to study French.

Most remembered was the way she taught.
My pronunciation was not good and she noticed.
She called me "Emile," I'll never forget
the way she would ask me to recite
a phrase, a sentence, and watch how I did it.
Leaning over her lectern, she would whisper,
"Emile, repeter, s'il vous plait."

It was her whisper that called us.
When she whispered to me, I felt it—
I felt her interest, her need for me
to say it clearly, correctly and to her.
Never mind my speech was so Southern
she had that way of saying I want you
to speak the language simply, directly.

My French was never good enough—
not for her but what I wanted for her.
Never unhappiness at my voiced struggle
but a pleasant way to show she cared.
It was her whispering that did it.
It was her whispering that made me want.

The Sign

It has come again,
the sign of real winter.
Out my door early,
I could not see across the street.
The cloudy thickness
made me cold and blocked
from going outside
in the midst of it.
When it comes,
I always imagine the world
at once covered
in a stilled pervasion,
extending its presence throughout.
I feel to step into it
would collect my soul
into a larger lost miasma,
something foreboding
and trackless.
Such short-lived fantasy
emerges with the appearance
of winter stillness.

When Time Came

When time came to choose
for him to decide,
what impulse brought her
to recall what was said,
as a reason to conclude?
What time will he commit
to stand with the others,
was the thought she mused,
not the yearly dues,
not the responsibilities.
Did he know where they were?
Did she pay attention?
He could see his friends
and those also there,
perhaps many like herself,
who knew very little
about all the reasons
for such loyalty
and accompanying fellowship.
Laughter and being noticed
seems to produce good feelings.
What reasons to listen.
But what means "to listen?"
Why do it?
Which comes first,
whether to have good reason,
or interpret what is seen
and match with experience,
if experience can resolve
what is said
from values undiscovered?
But what did it matter?
Just go with the feelings
and think from their warmth.
All persons are alone
until someone cares,

and how that is found
someone needs to share.
Where does it start?

Political Soundings

In the old inkwell seat—
scratched and deeply cut
on the top and on the sides
made it individual.
He was only one
among those in front and back
of the rectangular room.
They sat in line,
looking forward at her desk,
rebellious when she looked away.
Glances at each other
signaled the mischievous acts
to come with her book opened.
She hoped to read in silences—
theirs she hoped for study,
hers for time to read.
Whop! went a flattened sound,
and then came another
in succession,
but not simultaneous—
almost staccato
as if there were guns
going off in a scatter.
Up she came,
glasses removed in haste,
and down the rowed seats,
each with marred tops.
All sat in studied alertness,
waiting for one to be found—
lagging a careless mis-bump here,
an unintended nudge there.
She knew someone started,
some rabble leader.
But no one dared look
in his direction.
Her glance was stern.

The seaters sat in wonderment.
Angelic they looked
without a guilty clue.

Decades have passed
since those junior days
when struck the fearless leader,
breaking the hallowed silence,
soundings in the blocklike room.

I thought about it today
when noticing political runs
against established domains.
One office is filled
and held for elected term.
A new presence
must be noticed—
something different to cause
attention to be discovered
for all to question:
Who is this one?
Who comes to be?
The old seat to take
to give us all a stake
in what we might be.

Renditioned

Sitting in a room by oneself,
Everything still in its place,
One could assume, on the shelf—
Those things left one can trace
When thinking or looking to find
Apart from outside, a world designed.
The feeling or knowing with each item
That a human inhabits this space
With things inside belonging ad infinitum
To someone living or working in this place.
Windows to see outside can command
An occupant's attention, so out of stride
Where the life moves, distraction demands
The sitter to look where things collide
With the familiar stillness of things placed
Through lethargy, form is kept and traced.

Where is that form individual exacting
That is certain and personally positioned?
Does it betray or send such impacting
Notice of sameness from one's conditioned
Life to be a person living so renditioned?
Not unique with singular joys and preferences,
But distinguished for visitor's references?
To life as they know it, recognize it—
To be comfortable in a place not strange,
But cleverly expected with no furnishing change.

Going Somewhere

There is a world of people going somewhere.
Each morning brings forth a new direction—
Even though a new day's aims replace despair
Over answers unfound from studied detection,
Fresh moments in the offing are lying there
In wait to be used by hearts everywhere.

Modern life rides on wheels of a journey.
Each person moves out, facing the forward fray.
As each mind thinks, as if in a tourney,
Start together but travel onto a different way,
Depending on singular spirits and inclinations,
To achieve an end from known indications.

But where is the place called destination?
Is the day's trip a ride to a place,
Or a ride to the soul's last demarcation
From an imagined quest to find a trace
Of a lost path back to end a long distance
That will return a span from a given existence.

A Message Reclaimed

Some messages go away and some come again.
They return as if they have never gone away—
Some as if they were new and mark times to begin
Anew and called a season that's here to stay.
Decorations, music, and signs return and sway.
The atmosphere is made clear to awake and incline
A reason to swing about and move to go and seek.
Though the time is new, the times are old design.
People where they are tend to remove winter's bleak
Moments and know a story they choose to speak.

All greet the story's signal time of the year,
When fall has gone and winter will reappear,
Where each is struck by beauty of a clear night
That often comes when moisture forms of snow
Majestically come down, a gentle pleasure of sight.
All outside are moved to feel a reflective glow
When moonlight touches a stillness we all know.
And out of darkness comes a brightness-filled flow
That mounts buildings, earth, and trees that grow
With a temporary softness nature conceives to strow.

The message made clear, enhanced by the season
Draws us together, our minds dance the reason.
The meaning retold proclaims love to each other.
The bright light reminds of a time long past,
A past not lost but remembered to go further.
A past to be present in an act made to last.
The cold winter's evening is a virtual sign
To hold forth and find closeness to realign
With all people, all places to reclaim the design.

Beginning Winter Wind

The wind begins to blow between the trees.
Each winter limbs withstand the reaching cold,
Hinting that each one of us find the lees
Against the surge to rush in times foretold—
When to move with the stretching arms of time,
Gain one more chance to sing some loving rhyme.

The wind tells us with its calm-tempered blow
To quicken our spirits and open hearts to others.
Tidal lights beam forth from a tender flow
Each time we share with sisters and brothers
Words we give to care at the starting bend.
Like a sentient breeze, our love will transcend.

The season comes and moves our stifled hearts.
Past staid days now illumined with prisms of joy
Blown in delicate ways to give us starts
To renew all chances toward our employ.
Grace does come back in a heaven-sent way,
Which thrills our souls and reminds us to pray.

The beginnings again have come our way.
All feel the soft edge slipped by the trees,
A sign to us that a great voice did say,
"Love one another"—senses by degrees,
Given out as the wind touches all out there,
And moves to each other—the time is now here.

Had No Clue

His new fatigues bespoke his start.
He was just beginning his working art,
Waiting outside he stood alert
Till the other would come to insert
His claim to take a box of tools.
It had been said there were two fools
To be there in that kind of work.
His training had led him to this day.
He could not know this was not the way,
But he wanted to do it right.
All would be equal in their sight.
Some had gone to ride the tugs,
Others preferred to walk with mirthful shrugs.
Still he wanted to be a co-worker.
He really wasn't some kind of shirker—
A mechanic could not work without the tools;
He knew that from attending both the schools.
Soon all were gone out to the line.
He felt pretty dumb to take the time,
But he wanted to be fair and wait.
Finally the other came at a speedy gait;
Now did not matter the other was late.
Politely, he let the other be first to enter.
Two boxes on the floor were in the center.
One was old and bent and used.
And one was new, clean and unused.
The other lunged and grabbed the new.
He had waited and had no clue
The other would take such a view.

Searching Minds

Streaks of light pierce recesses like shards
That fly into once shadowy areas,
Unseen for periodic points of time,
And then the dark is lifted for bards
To write about daunting hysterias—
Mysteries sought for good words sublime.
Tales of horror infest searching minds
As inquiry feeds into lonely hearts.
The writers pose sagacious searches
As sherlockly keenness surely finds
Routes taken from such amazing starts
Through spaces where a clue besmirches
An otherwise perfect hideousness.
Soul-searching minds park in silent strath
To allow themselves concentration
To find a strange curiosity
On a deviously misgotten path—
Assays in mental constipation.

Here to Stay

Across the landscape there lies one sure thing.
Each dawn or evening break still to bring,
Whether one steps in firm or soft terrain,
Again the known place to stand will remain.
The solid ground each foot for its support
Needs to walk, sit or run for abode or port.
Many ways are made to change its texture;
Many shapes are made to form a fixture
That lifts it, lowers it for human plot.
It stays in any way its moved or not.
It holds our buildings as well as ourselves;
Yet it turns our thoughts when someone delves
Into the kinds of tools used to change
Its look, or emit such sounds to rearrange,
In holes or hills or slopes or beauty berms,
For purposes of use by persons or firms
With power or fame or money or game.

The earth was there before we humans came—
A place for us to share and live free;
But with common soil we still fail to see
The basic foundation we all must share,
To exist for normal life as pure air.

Flutes of Life

Moisture touches the plants, saturating their trunks and
    stems,
The procreant laying on of a soaking that will not all run off,
Penetrating through the bark of each perennial plant's limbs.
Even the escaping water eases into the soil as it troughs—
Mysterious obsolete drains carrying to their roots,
Where the almost last vestiges act as transverse flutes.

Some days the sky does not yield from its cloudy drains
The hydrogen-oxygen wetness so necessary for growth.
The all-living things continue contesting what remains
Of the liquid life-giving lubricant that sustains for both.
Soft life and dry death will be a test of their existence.
Nature's decision will invoke their required persistence.

Human life, not unaware of the vicissitudes to plant life,
Cannot go on from day to day with mere individual passivity,
Paying only aesthetic attention to all lurking natural strife.
Drawing parallels to the higher human chain sensitivity
Elevates each mortal's concentration on multiple dependence.
Life and death creates a recognition of general transcendence.

The tree out my window is God's best representation to us all.
It grows and droops and droops and grows with sun and rain.
One reduces its life when the other is absent its plying fall.
The radiance of each person's caring to cease all other's pain,
And the giving of sustenance when each need is stressed
Enlivens the living world importance when they are addressed.

Value of Place

Does it matter where we may be
When the light makes its last bright show?
When we scatter where we may see
To and from the range of its glow?

A gentle breeze brushes the flowers—
Their startled petals in last gasp,
Like little trees of succumbed bowers
Do not know what sustenance to ask.
Soon, very soon, the round light will go.
Will it end this time; no return
To hope again to search to know
And in between research the turn?

What value is it where to be
Before it will be the dark to last
Until the day will come so vast
When stretching eyes want no delay.

But do we need to find the place?
Do we need to have a point to see
When the sun covers all the space?
Need we not value where to be?

Dream Cantos

Though hard to know what feeds each mind,
What thinks a soul can reach its way
In all the forms of humankind
And be judge of each life's own stay.

The time of dreams gives rest to ease
And forms will be in the shadows,
Once again comes an old disease
When slumber's ache drives its cantos.

Afflicted dreams numerate fears.
Disturbed rhythms stop cognate rest.
One's daytime choices buried for years
Waking to consciousness a soul's test.

Unreasoned minds suffer their souls
When they let their lives harbor pain—
Sore thoughts invade psychic controls,
Driven in from some tortured gain.

What is felt is first touched income—
Messages rousing in those received,
Where past joys or hurts have come from,
Impact cognizances of that believed.

Compared to a once frightened contact—
A careless incident transpired.
Relief after all was not fact.
How deep was the memory mired?

Income choice may not be controlled—
Not able to sublimely select.
The effect like the sea unrolled
Can come in not as one would expect.

Mind lodgings difficult to forget,
As dream-flowing uncensored scenes,
Changes restful sleep into regret
And consciousness reasons for means.

When a deed or word was ill said,
Intention was a moment's spur,
A mental drub, a minor dread,
Wells in the sensitive to deter.

Release to rest a disturbed mind,
To ease the torment when self brought,
Divides a life that's been inclined
Between will and made troubled thought.

One side is love for complete life,
Love for each one who lives with all
And the engaged whose life is rife
With secret greed for other's fall.

What choice is made can lift us all,
Can find each day a chance to give.
No matter where, what verse written,
Life can be made where sweet dreams live.

Nothing to Prove

Those days when standing within a pictured arch,
Rehearsing on a platform, waiting to be told,
Being directed as if caught in one wide socket,
Head set for sound through the cochlea to march
When instructed to move up or down, plots unfold.
Thinking of the view for crowds to like or dislike,
Those days I was impaled as if by a shrike.

Are we players curtailed on a stage of life?
Like pets are we waiting for view removal—
For pet lovers seeking creatures in pounds—
Creatures from cages who wait on approval?
Are we waiting for others to make their rounds
To care and feed us and lift us out of our strife?

Can living be said to strive to make one's stamp,
A *sigillum* placed wherever there and when
Stages are set and crowds will dare not denounce?
Does the proscenium limit where steps tramp
Along the predicated path one needs to win
Until character glory grants time to announce?

Perhaps it can be true "all the world's a stage,"
But when to walk upon it, given the time:
Will it be like a lion's ferocious bite
At the moment when he finds prey to engage,
Or will the cat's meow suffer so sublime
That tender hearts will be stolen at the sight?

For a stage I strolled the river bank today;
On water's edge I saw a tall wading bird.
He stood on just one leg; the other folded.
Picture still his long neck did not give sway,
Nor did his long straight bill part a word,
Not a squawk. He was so still as if molded.
Startled at his being so close, I stood still too.
Such elegance had compelled me to just stare.

Resting or awaiting a fish, I knew not why.
Was he ignoring me, staking this place close?
To go further I dared not, for he might move.
The day was clear under a cloudless blue sky
And his complete self erect in regal pose—
His self was truly his with nothing to prove.

Maybe his whole stage with the sky his arch,
It occurred to me, did not depend on sound
Outside his ear to know where to go and when.
His stage was nature, no need of costumed starch.
From where did he come or where could he be bound?
My mind searched questions where I could begin.
Then I considered why did I need to know.
He came; he stood; he looked; he was there to be.
It was quite enough to have been there to see.

Suddenly, without anxiety, he moved.
As his other leg came down, he spread his flanks.
Under his great long wings, he approached the sky.
Slowly, smoothly he rose as though the air were grooved.
Not direct away at first, he glanced back in thanks.
I knew not how I came to think this or why.

Comfort Folds

Cold when to bed and colder in the early light.
The sky could not be seen through the wind-blocking tarp,
Only looked for when eye-peeking from the bulk covers
And then quickly back under the black warmth from sight;
Almost like the peerless blackness was some time warp,
Some prenatal return to a dream time from mothers.
Sleep was over but the cold back porch was a tomb,
Not a place to venture out into the morbid cold.
That deathly chasm on the bleak boards had to be crossed,
A journey to the kitchen door beyond this room.
To extract my frail young body made spirit bold,
The frozen gap of torture between heat and frost.
When the times come, one often hesitates to think—
Questions measure the distance a comfort must take.
Comfort is not continuous travel to itself.
There is now and again a trip made to the brink.
Contemplation can usurp a mind's troubled break
From the warmth secluded worth of one's recessed shelf.
Sleep-end consciousness turns the mind to broken day.
From one's own self-heat generated dark kingdom
Comes a retracing of last edging sight of night.
Day's decrease seems colder with frost's hoary display.
The grass moistness starts its coverage of turfdom
And the softened crust makes sparkle the evening light.
The backyard behind the slumber porch's wintry lot,
With its wooden fenced-in signs of inclusive use,
Rests in the mind's last seeing of day's work remnants.
An oak pile fresh cut lies in the center spot
Against which leans a double-bit axe amid refuse—
Shavings and hunks of wood split through by implement.
Thoughts of climbing to the top of the pile to play
King-of-the-Hill games to seize the day in conquest—
Child's play in preparation for life's triumphant goals.
Thoughts' lingering moments succumb to dream's way
As then the day's end fades completely into night.
The growing warmth is encompassed a returning guest
That finds no more the need to stretch the comfort folds.

The Way It Goes

Out the door engulfed by the darkened night,
Unsteady steps probing for reflections,
Feeling for physical touch absent sight,
Rain's wetness ensconces night's inspections.
Were not the lighting of a sightless way
By flooding roads for all who want to see,
And be touched by the rain hidden from day,
And know from feel and sight the world can be,
Then each forward march what history shows
Would not have come down that way long ago,
And now descends—that's the way it goes.

The spattered pool beside the curb reflects,
From thrown streetlight glow, evidence of rain
Dark nights hide if not for little specks
Bubbling like a cauldron's exhausted strain.
Except from overhead drops, placid within,
The water's face spreads with circles again,
And again like tiny majestic upheavals.
Quickly vanishing as if were primeval—
As once when earth was in climatic throes,
They came down that way in times long ago,
And recur once more—that's the way it goes.

Night does not stop raindrops piercing through,
Touching or seen by a glimmering space light,
To their striking place bent by the wind askew,
They become trapped from their downward flight.
Free from concern for any surface where they land,
Ending their erratic direction; they flop,
Echoing flat sounds as were trapped by hand.
They are crushed when their rushing journeys stop.
Touch, sight or sound, liquid water then flows.
They came down that way in times long ago.
And in time escaped—that's the way it goes.

The sealed bulb lights on poles help us explore,
As once when gas lights did pervade the streets
To give us less groping to search for more—
For more space, more passage, for less retreats,
For knowing directions to overcome defeats.
Walking off to find more places to learn
More roads to make our way through the nights,
Lighting the blinding darkness to discern,
To expand beyond, to enlarge our sights.
The mind unlike the rain, which the wind blows
In moving learns—that's the way it goes.

As the veil turns the symbol of the dark
When both dispel light's escaping clarity,
Like the protected voyage of the Ark,
Will and reach seemed such a disparity.
By the voyage stirred great adventure
That a cover seemed a needed element,
Where the journey ends should make the venture
And reveal oneself in soul development
To go where the mind can be led to go
And the heart will light the way the mind knows
That spirit insights—that's the way it goes.

Many lights offer the ways to declare
The mind's eye to the things known and unknown.
All roads do not lead back to once despair,
Frequent return route treks to days foregone;
But to fresh enlightenment newly displayed,
At times the light does not touch the mental night
And the soul's mystery seems so delayed,
And the joy of finding is not clear or right,
For the hunger of expansion light bestows,
And the steps toward clarity not bright,
But the search is worth—that's the way it goes.

To stroll the evening streets place to place,
Ever searching for new enlightenment,
Fosters self-help in coming face to face,
Coming upon what will restore excitement.
The night magnifies the oneness to search,
Not knowing what may be breached ahead,
Being drawn through the covering reminder
That which may not be seen helps go where led,
Where next greeted by the unknown splendor.
Steps through streets drawing wonder and suppose
What will come next—that's the way it goes.

Advances to find replaces known haunts,
Which persist in the present known mind.
The way gone before eases insecure taunts,
But what is learned from nothing left to find?
Seeking souls cannot rest from each return.
Wandering through the lights to eternity,
They must travel the channel of concern
Where rests the amalgam fraternity.
Therein that territory without bound
Lies beyond all the known places yet found.
And there dwells the ultimate holy ground.

Come Back

There are no shadows found in darkest night.
No sparkle condescends the dignity.
Ingracious mystery affords no sights
For wandering eyes—no propensity
To discover what reception might seek.

Sleep prevents any period distraction;
Wayward proclivities quite bleak,
Leaving all worldly things to impaction.
But night is not referenced right away.
Closure comes after lingering light fades—
That instant tightens in an obscure way,
As all acts are shut out by tender shades.

The last remnants of prosecutorial day,
For a time revived only in the mind,
Become flashes with so much to defray—
Like rational expenses gone blind,
Engineered to eradicate circumstances
After thoughts slip together unrefined
And uncensored to destroy all fences.

By volition there are no stars to see.
The human switch tries to click out the time.
The day dissolves into so much debris—
Leftover thoughts, feelings with no rule or rhyme.
Then comes into this meandering mix—

A dream crowded, unclear, striving to be free.
Like a clock that monotonously ticks
An idea looms, escaping memory;
Yet, not clear, it struggles amid the seams
To rise back into the light of reason.

What a dilemma to restore with a dream!
Between soothing sleep and cluttered treason,
Human restoration from the dullish dark
Mired in the uneven flow of diverse things,
A wellspring of growth, no matter how stark,
Arises to endow life with the joys it brings.
One night ago from tired throes of the day
When sleep was welcomed and dreams once more sought,
That dark nobility was invited to give his way.
Let me come there to put aside fights fought,
Rest myself in perhaps a pleasant dream.
Not knowing how long, soon came this flowing stream.
It was made of clouds that seemed on display.
And I, in the middle, drew everyone's attention.
As this fusion of unreason began,
And the day's credence no longer retention,
My life became creative, fears soon ran.
Self-expression made my being alone
In a world without restriction and loss
A sense of succeeding where life was soft
And turmoil from the past day was soon gone.

When back the day came and filled with reason,
The dream comfort returned a new approach.
Feelings were refreshed as if a season
Had come back and now life without reproach.

A Wanting Spell

Somehow dreary days cast a wanting spell,
So many birds missing from a cloudy sky.
Seems impossible to warm necks and backs.
Now and then makes one shudder a little,
Trying to increase the body heat lost.
Drizzling rain comes down absent a warm flare,
Makes the heat inside not right in the air.

As a child it was confining held inside,
Having to have something to hold the mind—
So hampered by walls while outside could find
An openness more suited for life and search,
As if wonders of God were just outside
When the world exposed was not known inside—
Could reveal the urge for not being trapped
When the young need to search and seek newness.
The old was seen every day as if unwrapped.
It was hard to feel real unvarnished wind.
In the artificial world of heating vents,
Amid the sameness of furniture placed—
Always in the same spot, no new intents.

That contrast was so vivid and straight-laced
Would that the outside were in and in out.
If both could be mutually inclusive,
Then what feelings would attribute adventure;
So then longings of youth would not exist
And the wonders of the world not persist?

His Own Design

Life was seen only from his point of view,
Like the lake fish he knew swimming through
The brackish water had to be fished each day anew.

He knew, or thought so, life was just like fishing:
The place had no more covering than to be swishing
Through the water that squeezed his dip net meshing.

Not a tall man but just the size to float home.
Home was where he knew his paddled foam.
His short arms strong enough to guide him across alone.

He couldn't wait to get back from the job each day.
Running from the garage to the back steps was play.
The last of the day had come for him to get away.

Putting on his fishing clothes as fast as he could,
He was out to hitch his little boat each day so he would
Drive to his lake to catch the fish he should.

Backing his boat down to the water finds a ditch—
It sloped down just below his hitch,
Leaving the car, he and boat scratched the water's itch.

Always across to the other side where he knew they were.
Rubbing around the cypress knees, he made them stir.
He knew just the top to water bait, just the right lure.

Such happiness was there for him to always find.
Life was so simple and interesting, both in kind.
A place, a time, made to suit his design.

Chronicle Markers

Time goes by without a look at the sky
Except when to pause and see it's fair,
Or cumulus clouds heap and multiply
So that one feels to test the cooler air.
Luminescence wakes us not every day
To the brilliance we can identify,
Even though the light shed is on display;
And the things reflected we do not see:
That Gregorian timepiece, the star sun;
Sailboats in the bay cupping wind at sea;
Tree fields under mountaintop's silver run;
At shrinking day the lone appearing moon
In its celestial orbit of the earth.
Following comes the visual suit, soon
To test the lunar voyage of light's worth,
Attention to the equivalent day.
Chronicle markers measure our life's span,
Remind us of periods going by,
And gently, slowly tell us of human
Spacers or life, chances to teach us why
Time is short with peaks of grace to live.

Today, noticing thc Olympic peaks,
A child heard me remark on what I saw:
"Oh, such a sight! Could stare at them for weeks.
If I did, there would not be any work done."
Then the child said, "We don't use them very much."

A Poet's Rapture

Kind of world it will be today
Drew me to look through the front pane,
As if that would tell me the way
To discover what human gain.
The smooth warm sheets held my being
No longer from escaping dreams
And exploring options, seeing
Something that would define the seams.
Cross the streets and through a prism,
Between two similar objects,
The sound with whitecaps formed a schism:
Contemplation to find subjects,
To compose a furrow to link,
A means of contact with still words,
Words as pathways to help me think.
What was there was there except birds.
They awake with the light and dart
From one aim to what they find next.
Days come, not bothered with a start,
They flit from one thing to any fixed
Thing, there to surmise and fly on.
The poet must exceed each rapture
As if the world was all his zone
Where to search and flit and capture
The essence of how things relate:
Beyond why seas roll in the wind;
Why birds fly such a rapid rate;
Or when we break when need to bend.

Distracting Clout

The seat slid into had no uncertain punch
On my back or bottom to take notice—
No such bump, or loose stitch to make me hunch
Forward or shift my weight forward or back.
When my coat bunched around my tailbone,
I knew that would not do but adjust.
Since my glasses shifted, another moan
To get ready, get settled, knew I must
Get comfortable before starting out.
Such need for the pure thought you always stop;
You take care of what it is that has clout,
That has the power to distract, to slop
Into your mind the freedom to clear think.
All these cells to wipe out other beeps
That short-circuit like a synaptic wink.
How we wish for peace, release from the top
So that the cellular case we must hold
Within to use for controlling our travel—
The undisturbed inner matter going bold
Through equations of life to unravel
Without pushes' and shoves' external gnaws,
Place on each cerebrum's purposeful pause.

Repose

Breathless calm erodes the fitful day.
Blackened cloth drapes the seamy stance
Formed from all the rearranging fray
That excites drives for one more chance.
A blanket of stillness provokes
A time to pause, reconnoiter
What next discovery life evokes
In the embroidery after.
Conversations stir the ego,
Fire's smoking winds of self-belief.
Children play until wants outgrow
Momentary pain's anxious relief
And night subsides in hidden flow.
Sounds off are made without seeing
The cars, the rain, the chatter muffed
Give a different outline being
Considered for new meaning fluffed
Like a pillow reshaped to fit
For sleep's reserve to grant surcease.
The mind's ideas become split
In recovering dreams of peace.
Strange connections' rhythmic nuances
Seem normal reactions to take
With known and unknown influences
Converging for slumber's sake.
But all this when dream's unconscious
Casts out the restrictive censor
Will the cover from day's conscious
Rest the mind from life's demeanor.

Spirits Swell

A town circle displaying the Sound;
Small shops separating door to door
With a fountain in the middle,
Hesitates the comer to go around.
Then down to the ferry explore,
Hopefully, a tourist place to fiddle.
All traffic is drawn west to face
The sea and view the ships sail by.
Restaurants hover the beach front.
Boardwalking to the mariner's place
In the scheme where sea gulls fly.
Right and left one won't be errant
In this quite small attractive trace.
They come to see and, easily led,
They find an escape from the city.
Drawn to a closer looking place,
Some want to stay and it is said
A condo to live life so pretty.
So quite small become not so small.
Built on hills that overlook the sea,
And needing for many to see
Over others who must have it all;
Multi-levels grow more to be
For those who closer inevitably
Will have their new life fulfilled.
So what is a view but a dream
Of being where feelings can dwell.
And life is a search of place willed;
And life found in a drawing scheme;
And plotted plans make spirits swell.

Now History

They were never too close.
Now under the cold mounds,
she came long after him,
no one now to go by and see
where they were left.
Among many others beside
a little road winding back
into the woods farther,
they lie side by side,
Off from this patch
of sites a highway runs
through a town grown up.
The old haunts still there
but no longer living.
Some are historic places,
they call them, standing.
The town has shifted
to where the malls are.
New factories have come
bringing more trucks
to haul goods away
to many different places.
New homes make up
new areas of growth.
Years, decades have passed
and the mounds still there
with buried little markers.
Addresses of loved ones
moved away who knows
where have made their
lives in among other malls.

Around the old town
where once were fields
of cotton and gins,
pine trees grew up.
Long straight concrete strips
separated by a grass ditch
busily hum from tires
going and passing that way.
What used to be there
snuggled into agriculture
has become consolidated.
Restaurants, service stations,
and new lives around malls.
Crisp new store fronts
planned and placed in asphalt
are now the gatherings—
Multi-plex movie theatres
hardware and grocery
stores next to each other,
mortuary across the street.
In another part of town
the old oak trees stand
jutting their massive limbs,
shading the now history—
landmarks for someone.
Someone left may remember.

Choices

The most precious ability is choice,
Choice to believe or reserve a belief
Itself a decision whether or not to voice
Until some thought to explore or conceive.
So many thoughts daily bring their toll
On the mind to ingest, reconnoiter after.
So many groups solicit being on their roll,
Offer their central aims; accept their character:
What one must pay or agree to do,
Yet called volunteer to activate this project,
Equates to the thought or feeling, see it through
And reap motto rewards fulfilling an object.
Persons seem to know, pledge their thinking
And smile and say you are one of their own.
Exquisite loyal contact leaves doubt shrinking
While the work of working leaves none alone.
Reason is engineered through values
When youthful days' education forms action,
Which only growth and expectation imbues
To favor choices made in transaction.
Bargains are made when rewards are projected
That suit the self presently affected.
Living and working without the self connected
Will never be a surfeit to claims expected.

Flight of Fear

The sun of my life was not always
streaming into my heart warm with love.
Air's cold flooded spiritualless
when its deepening blanched my young soul.
Play was a torrential escape route
to lose the manufacture of fears
grown in the family upbringing.
Kicking the pigskin orbiting space
giving an extension-forced release
was the hero seeking world acclaim.
Direction sought become uppermost
as if contact energy jarred me.
The enveloping sky gave freedom
to stretch my life into devouring
atmospheres, penetrating life's shrouds.
In that present death of limitless
dreams, play was not play done to amuse;
but to break free, open to heaven's
space, flying to the sun's enchantment.

Flights of Fusion

The soft feel of the carpet nap
begs my feet take another step
into your world, which does not spin
but comforts my abstract measures.
You let me climb like an eagle,
at times soaring cliffs of ecstasy,
at other times capturing winds
of direction by letting my feet
be undisturbed flights of fusion.
Flowers do not grow; they open.
Clouds do not fly over; they drift.
Birds do not fly; they flit and soar.
To see the connection of things
allowed to elope my mind,
through the stylus to the paper,
like the hummingbird's pendular
motion that succulent moment
when the creative need is drawn,
you are there to accept my dream.
With the morning's start of the day,
as the sun draws moisture away,
the essence left is your supply.

Wait

Went today to renew my license—
To do the common thing on time.
Once again to stand in line, to sense
The wait and patience to resign
Oneself to pay the fee, take the tab.
Saw a neighbor and gave a smile.
Into my eyes he sent back a jab.
Satisfied, at least, had some style;
Then while there in wait to be next,
Another came to assume a place
In line with a pleasant look fixed
To do the deed in a meaning face.
I spoke, she spoke, both were friends.
Some old and new was what we knew.
Sometimes the wait can have good ends:
Lives renewed, regained life through.

Intention

A villain exhorts his limiting power,
Which controls the life of others, extends
Over even instincts. Like a tower
Stands from his ultimate use apprehends.

My mind construes what machinery gives
When my reason maintains for my choices,
Yet within all my mental storage lives
Those preconstructed commanding voices.

A crow and a sunken puddle did connect
When a dropped French fry found was too salty.
In the water and out, he beaked to inspect
To clear his hunger when food proved faulty.

When humans devise, what creatures can test?
Life for all includes vast knowledge acquired.
Although motives propel us do our best,
Effects unexplored may harm those inspired.

All things to be used from the earth's supply,
All thoughts translated and made to live free,
Whether words there are for meanings to try,
Existence is *tam facti quam animi*
(as much in deed as in intention).

Delay

Too early to wake up, she's still sleeping.
The pillow is still soft.
My tired eyes are weeping.
Starlight breaks through the window aloft.

Her drowsy face puffs. How soft her breaths.
There's warmth over there.
My hand would caress,
But the night is too young to spare.

My mind won't let me sleep. Can't turn or toss,
The bed might move.
Her night would be a loss.
She seems so settled in her groove.

My dreams are no longer. Too soon wide awake
Where have they gone?
Be still for her sake.
Were not for her there, I'd be alone.

Too late to sleep again. Spend myself waiting,
Caught between night and day,
Hearing myself respirating.
Life oftentimes is waiting out delay.

A Song to Insight

Still the light has not come to force the day.
The felt foot starts a search to find the way.
Soles press first to seal the touch, uncertain
Of all the surface that might hold the weight.
A strange call to stalk a thickened curtain
Pulls at the soul as if it could not wait
To flee the stain to be not in any one place.
Strange pull to walk out on the smooth pavement
With the bathing dampness soft on the face.
This outside look before daylight, darkness
Gives anticipation, yet draws amazement—
Something there to find in the black starkness.

The night is also steeped in the grog of fog—
That lack of sight that dispels a clear head.
No wish to be is dimmed by solar slog
That clears the sleep from a slumbered bed.
Something to find in a fog sleepless night.
Something to know without life's distractions.
The stilting fog holds back the missing light.
Fear need not prevent free satisfactions
Of the self to think without a flurry
Of problems, other's thoughts, another's worry.
Foggy nights can be a song to insight.

The mind is pure to find what the self knows;
The mind and the heart absent the civil blows.

Someone's of Us

We have a daughter; her name is Beth.
If were a son, could be Bob or Seth.
We remember her little child's legs
And her light hair, so thin it was.
And her eyes, yes, still are something—
They noticed everything.

For some a change growth does make.
From a child grew a smart lady,
Now developed into a loving mother.
To us same Beth, new legs, same eyes.

What a beauty she was and is—
Someone's of us to love is there.
Someone's of life to breathe the air.
New legs, new hair.
But same Beth, noticed everything.

Once let slip away in a store.
Not too far, we could see.
She knew we would not let her go.
Let her go; let her go—
Does change make growth?
Away from us she has gone.
Smart lady now a mother—
Someone's of us to love is there.
Gift of life to breathe the air.

Saw a little girl the other day,
Watched her walk, looked the same way.
Could her name be Beth?
She noticed everything—
Someone's of us to love is there.

Down the Street

The old man walked upright down the street.
His head was high and his eyes straight ahead.
His face seemed to press forward replete
With a countenance looking fully fed
By a clear life free from pain or sorrow.
As he today could find joy tomorrow,
And every day to walk so never to borrow
Or need the esteem from any other alive.
With his old-fashioned felt hat and red tie
In front of a starched collar, he would derive
The noble thrust of self anywhere to ply
His life to any place his proud soul would try.
It was hard to tell his need for the cane.
He seemed with its touch, he did not rely
On it to brace his weight or search a plane
To direct his course where he had to walk.
More than once he stopped for someone he knew—
Someone who gave his name to start a talk.
Each time his body, his hands would construe
Such gestures to the other that he could review
The points made almost without use of words.

Looking up in the sky, I saw some birds.
At times they would turn the same direction,
Each time circus performers on the trapeze
In midair catch hands with such perfection.
We stare at the birds' and the artists' ease.
Birds fly together and we know not why.
Artists train their bodies without need to see.

There is such promise but we cannot fly
Like the birds and everywhere try to be—
To react without voice or eyes to tell.

In the world a soul somewhere starts as well.
To learn is to find oneness to dwell.

A Wingless Morrow

This kind of day is made to fly.
The plane is there against the sky.
From earth's gee fix, we now must try
A trip above we cannot deny.
Is it an act we do not know
That tells our soul we now must go
Away from all the anchored stands
Of all the needs, requests, demands?
Beyond the pull, beyond the greed,
Beyond the search, beyond the need
To have control, to leave the drudge,
Where one can find no cause to budge.

Release the brakes, push the throttle.
The speed increases, buoys like a bottle.
Afloat is felt, a rush of air—
Noses up above and comes aware
That earth has no longer a stair.
No looking back; clear to ascend.
The ease is there, we will extend.
Between life and death no sorrow
Can slip by the wingless morrow.
No need or force to further wait
For wealth or things to clear the slate.
A time when life's a clear review;
But nothing holds a backward view.
And earth no longer needs a stair.

Discover

The air can be heard wiping the panels blowing by.
Sometimes the trucks' tires want to stick to the pavement;
But they spin so fast they only give a licking sound,
Albeit the wetness from last night's rain free their
    enslavement.
They race along whenever their touch is forced aground.
From my studying place, they now and again tell me I must
    rely.
The light above my head blinks and tells me the current draw
Is teased by some slight disturbance that accents its steady
    flow.
Comfort found in my leather chair captures my staying place,
Allowing myself to let me wonder of locales to go.
My desk will hold my concentration on the human race
With clear and less abrupt ways to examine through less flaw
In all the translated sounds I make from life's productive
    world.
There are so many things we utilize to call upon for living:
The transportation and the sources of power tear us away
So much that we seek each day what those things are giving,
So much so that those things we think we need gain more
    sway.
My soft chair and clear lighting fools me as they become
    unfurled.
Where is the wisdom to clear my head and help me know my
    toil—
On one hand help me explore what is most important each day,
What is best to occupy my mind while seeking the material?
The time to think and the time to feel, aloof from all display,
With the grace that I will discover a chance for the ethereal
And all the things that seem so important I may soon uncoil.

I once knew a man who searched to find what he could give.
Somehow he did not know that his reach was how we would
    live.
Though he had great skills to make his physical life secure,
He found how to both make things and control the product
    lure.
More important were all others with whom he tried to contact
For the ways he could lend himself to them for their impact.
His great gifts became clear to all who grasped his presence,
And knew their lives to prosper when they found his essence.

Her Essence

Not one thing is so sweet as the first light
When it on verge of day disarms the night.
The unseen fear gives way its shortened stay
Each time it strums the petals and breaks the day,
Warms the grass and dew and slumbering flowers,
Not yet in need of spring's gentle showers.
So much do I want for that edge to turn
From the brink of sad dreams to joy, to learn.
I have someone to take my troubled heart
And hold it in her hand for one more start.
Once more does resume her saving presence,
As her clearing sweetness brings her essence
Of what others can be and all will be
If I could but just view more than I see.
And then the place for us is not a void,
Is now love-softened for both employed
In having the spirit-freeing soul to live
With others making roads to find, to give.

Values Reflected

The time came to go and everyone went to their cars,
All on one side of the street; all at rest in a single row.
With "see ya later" waves to marches for other stars,
All keyed their doors and started cars ready to go.
As I put my key to engage the switch, nothing stirred,
No turn of the starter, no hint that the car would start.
Others were passing by as I found no way to depart.
Then a friend came up to see what had occurred,
Since I was still there while others had peeled away.
In short, we found a jumper cable would be needed.
To his car and back with battery power he would supply.
My battery was tied to his and keyed motion repeated.
The kindness a friend gave, upon whom I could rely,
Was there when from him I found he truly was my friend.
When we unbolted the wire, I saw a quite new cable—
No grease left on my hands nor on the other cable end.
This drew my notice to the neatness of care he was able
To have. A spotless car he had driven for many a year.
It made me think of him and what I knew and now revere—
A clean man and fitted in both what he wore and said.

Values are more than our ideals we have or once read.
Something in the patterns of all natures live in the head,
Which come into us from beliefs or religions so freely held,
Which come from everything we do, resists as a firm weld
The stresses and strains that may be heard in daily woes
To strive always when it would be easier in daily throes,
To be careless and short-circuited as if a waste of time
Can come from little chores reflecting another life sublime.

Search or Sanctity

The air is sprayed by the pummeling purity of rain showers.
Blinking, sometimes you look to see the unreadable,
Like the pelting one takes from some authoritative hosing
    powers
That being on the wrong end makes you often wonder why.
A walk in the rain, careless of any belligerent soaking spate
Received somehow someway, deludes the thinking to satiate
The claims to overcome what society has said for years,
"Get out of the rain; you can see you're getting wet."
But what does anyone know about why one steers
A life in spite of all saliva-splashing scolding you've met?
Stride on upright in the splattering, spirit-drenching clarity.
In spite of all the "know not to" haunting severity
Of meanings known only to the dried-behind-the-ears
    purveyor,
Who knows only his tired estimates of why one decides
To do something, as if the truth were only in the surveyor.
There is a fresh cleansing quality in all that abides
Within one's selfhood that enlivens and freshens the soul.
The search or the sanctity of it is one's own mark or goal.

Another Story

Rubbing the blinds, lighting the warmth of day,
Comes through tears in the draping night, unseen
To the human eye, but like a thick spray
That has a silent speed drifting serene—
Unable to be caught in instant glory
For what we term the day, another story.

First to see through parting lids for each one—
Just true from each breaking crack in blind sleep
An edge to dreams and perception is won.
Let go that mist of night, a reaping kind.
Newness to unravel between conscious
Schisms of right and wrong to what is sententious.

Dreams linger from such strong fading away.
To hold on to delight, resisting time,
Stop the light and prevent the break of day
And will to stay behind to dream sublime.
When a rested body urges stay awake
Then find the courage of the day to take.

All sheets are thrown back and ache of still rest,
Now must force a turn from internal musings.
The return to reason, no matter the test
Becomes real for life going on confusing.
The trail of dreams quickly slips into the day,
Eclipsed without even a wail gone astray.

Their Island Trace

A mynah bird flew up and landed firm
On the palm frond just off my landing,
As the staunch ocean breeze's gusty term
Gave the rooftops their early blown sanding.
The daylight gradually came in pale blue
Streaked across the sky for a fixed hue.

I could not remove myself away to go
Find the life awaiting the coming day.
Opening this way with all the beauteous flow
Made me not want to escape such display—
As if God drew this painting just for me
To begin and say, "Pause and pray and see."

But then no song comes your way to stay.
Friends await, a schedule must be kept.
Their love will surely share more sweet array
To give of themselves as such balm has swept
Our hearts and minds to grasp their tropic place,
And share their joys with us—their island trace.

Came time to leave this short-lived wonder.
Our thanks so inept, so simple for their gift
Of joy to be with us, we could not ponder
What to say, for their grace was our brief lift.
Somewhere in us when friends freely give
Will remain our love for their help to live.

Life's Air Goes

The breath of life seeps from an unknown source—
Weeps from a place fraught with true speed and force.
Unseen wings float it into widest scope
To be found wherever it has vital need.
The want of it drags from space silent speed.
It is a vital wonder of each life—
A strength to exist when lost causes strife.
A rich treasure sought when no longer there,
Once had and drawn upon when none to spare
Breaks the span of unconscious existence.
The worth of it takes on most persistence
When that fear not pervade it given measure,
Allowed importance to granted pleasure
Becomes pressed only when death is near,
And sneaks upon life becomes not clear,
Or that what was seems to leave what was here.
So then one knows free life comes no freer.

Not Remote

Ever start the day with your feet firm on watch?
Place found where the stand was held to see both
Up and down two streets, as the wake of day
Caught the first to be on the move to scotch
The first sale of goods to add that first loaf
Of bread on the shelves to start the first way
Into the food to have fresh to take home—
Take the first look as if were a new tome
To be for a scribe to reach, like a comb,
Each stretch of life to notch a day for all
Could be made clear, and not take for granted
The same of each day that posits the week,
The year that must be done to make a trace.
Ever think the start must be made, the first crawl
Up the street, into the store implanted,
So to fill a need, like a seed to tweak
The sight and smell of goods to shop and seek?

So important but yet near and common—
That failure to notice and try summon
Minds to dwell on words to write and describe
In such work for all to know and prescribe
To whom must have respect and all note
That to exist, we find others devote
Their lives so that we make them not remote.

Piercing Relief

A sheet of color devolved from the fading sunlit sky,
First seen through magnetic eyes, which cannot turn away,
Like a sheath momentarily releasing for a last array.

Hold on, hold on, for such beauty does not pass from us.
Such a strip of heaven astonishes the retaining days,
For a moment my eclipsed mind releases its problemed ways.

Such an instant is short-lived to pierce the consciousness.
Needs and wants are severed from its touching flash,
Touched are we from its brilliant multicolored slash.

Before and after its unrolling sweep into my eyes,
The up and down existence is torn to an even keel.
Held in its stream of grace extricates how one will feel.

Then, as it begins to change when a difference is noted,
Insightful awareness just as reaching slowly returns,
And reflection becomes a mental trace as twilight burns.

Look around and walk away is the common thing done.
Another glance back, but then, it is mysteriously gone—
Another reality has been shifted to be again alone.

Alone as we all are inside our thoughts to manifest;
But for a short time like a rapier, it came in.
Bless this phenomena for its out into there, when—

Her Heart Still Here

Coming across the street that sunny afternoon
Beside and between the sturdy old brick halls,
My heart hung with the hope of knowing her soon.
Old trees stood there too, fronting stately walls,
Making their green leaves reactions to spring days
As they fluttered, showing slightly a soft breeze.
Days of youth learning and promising new ways
Flowing in and through minds and spirits like trees,
Which grow unnoticed unless they speak promise
For nuanced eyes to see their majestic stance.
Sidewalks below shone from some sunlight pumice.
It was the approach from which caused my glance—
Her feign-free walk and well-combed clean blond hair
With bows of leaves over her reflected face,
Under which this sweet person made me declare.

We cannot go back to this clear holy place,
But our lives now, as they remain today,
Make hearts even more mature, fonder with His grace.
Hold the trees, leaves, and walks still, our love will stay.
Her life, her faith, her heart still here Mother's Day.

Than Being

When early I wake up,
The morning is not yet
A pass-through happening.
That moment is not there,
So do I await its glory,
Or do I go prepare
To start it with a piece
Of my life's constructions?
Whatever I do before,
If I lie awake to seek,
Will I include you, too
In my sequential start?
With me find joy today.
Let me think about you
And include in my dreams
All you are and can be.
The spark of your spirit,
Insert it in my life,
And want it to give me
A chance to live your dreams
As part of mine in love
Of being just together—
Nothing more than being
A sharing loving world.

Whose Space?

Like my floor fan, the blades run, their speed turns.
The air flow goes in a stream of felt wind
With every gush the pulse sends my body learns
To reduce the heat and restore a trend
Of normal heartbeat that again this once
Returns my turgid tissue to shrink back.
The frame moves to a task of quick response
Only to take again a calmer track,
Which sought the churned ease of twisted air.
How fast our new age takes control of life—
We cannot wait to make our own repair
With means we buy and feel the none contrite
As long as we can move as we wish.
Once was suggested that our space we rent.
From whom do we owe for this welcome dish
Of cool air we used to make ourselves content?

Machined Commotion

When first I passed her, driving fast down the street,
The day was clear and the usual world spun.
My route was short, one I needed to repeat.
I know not why I noticed her on my run—
Why I thought about her and her stately stare.
She stood tall, wearing a raincoat, collar up
To a lean face, glasses under her white hair.
Was it her bright face held so erectly up,
As she strode in lengthy stretch with a black cane?
Her pace was slow, and visage—a silent train
Evenly and slowly down on track without strain.

The time will come, I thought, all must slow their pace.
But keep pace we strive to reach from here to there;
Or else, lest we go and must limit our space.
Even our machinery speed becomes too fast;
So our bodies slow down, but our minds slip past.

When I came back, she had stopped so, filling
Her eyes, staring and seeming not to be tired.
Slowing my speed I saw her lodged, willing
To stand and look at something, though inspired;
So straight and focused on something down the street.
I somehow came aware, nimble life, too fleet.

On forward I went, glancing in my mirror.
On she went from a pause to refresh her mind.
She, on in her steady observing motion,
And I, I forward in machine commotion.

The Drawn Thought

Stand on a high place and look down on a throng.
The size can be seen in ways to capture thought.
High looks not often taken cause to prolong
The view to make the sense converge so taught
That minds' eyes will search out more narrow subjects.
Once found these sights enclose in a peopled trance.
There away we group our views in standout ways:
Over there are two young lovers with clasped hands,
Or down there are players, a musical band.
Near the bush is a painter musing his scene.
By the stream groups are walking, searching the water.
Many groups and singles become a visual screen,
An image, a great distant reconnoiter.
Which view, which viewer may spy longer which sight?
The high look may not last but what pulls it.
The mind observes the mind in its own drawn light.
The high place is but a span where eyes may sit.

Reflection

Across from skyscrapers reflecting their cloistered eminence,
A large waterway shimmers its beauty from the morning light.
Driving down the west highway succors a timely remembrance,
A visual photogenic display hard to draw away from sight.
Several miles separate the road from the beaming city.
A large bay provides useful commerce and dramatic pleasure.
On the parallel street, people saunter in magnetic felicity
As they stroll and feel the sun reflecting this expansive
    treasure.
People choose to reside on the sunward side of the road.
Bicycling and walking in the other side near the bay
Give the sense of a resort for languishing in a relaxed mode,
Enjoying the sounds and ambience of living the relaxed way.

Such lives, which exist and thrive in such open and tranquil
    passivity,
Are reluctant to change when surroundings normalize this
    appearance
When the place seems to be measured by such exclusivity,
The world moves on, with their lives unable to reconcile
    transference.

Slip the Day

Young minds make moves and glance around.
They cannot stand still even at work,
For even the walls unsettle their ground
When the eyes search for every little quirk—
Someone walks by, they will not fail to try
To find certain parts that interest them most.
A room becomes a scene they can supply
Their own plot to relieve boredom's host.
To move is more compelling to find anew
What was there before but now of use
To bring again some joy of what's true
To their world to be more than a ruse.
Still some work may eventually be done
Though unexciting it seems to be.
Meanwhile minds find places to run
Amid the fences they climb to see,
Where they can make all the rooms their own,
And fit themselves where they want to fit,
To gain the life their too certain day
From chairs to corner places to sit.
And somehow find time to slip the day.

Heart's Demands

How easy it is to give your heart away
To causes, to people, to books, to lesser things.
It's either heartfelt, heart-given, or heartless.
So soon to find the moment to let it stray—
A touching point, so well timed to loose the strings
Held to common thought for some inspired noblesse.

We find ourselves moved by something to share—
A happening, an event, a moment granting
All of us a chance to feel the depth of life—
We feel the sense that livens us to declare
The water, the sky, the forest so enchanting
That our spirits are lifted to filling our life.

Sometimes our senses are deadened by some acts,
Some things we see, or hear that reverse our hopes,
That penalizes, that deflates our good dreams
To want beauty and justice to devolve hard facts,
With the ugly and unjust reduced in our scopes,
Then cruel realities shall not detain our dreams.
Today I saw a man whose heart had given out.
Medical persons came and revived his breath.
How long he has now was placed in others' hands.
His heart now must be helped to keep life's bout
With life given to hope until time to rest.
What can we give to make life worth what life demands?

Choice

As the smoke-gray fog tufted the cold gray air,
Its sealing act donned a beard like an ambit,
Reached the sky's edge in calm secret to declare:
Remain, do not search beyond, quiet your trumpet;
Match not this ceiling signal of another place,
Another world of its own time and distance.
Turn your face of no sense private concerned space
To have no heed to delve with such persistence.
Perceive your own created, detached bright light,
And in this brilliance let this covering conceal
The range it has found to live in its own right,
Within its own realm to exist and to feel.
One day this disguise will be loosened, free
To be shaved away as if it came and went,
Discarded away to change its will to see.
And growth shall be by volitional consent.

Someone Else

Who would be smart with a mind not revealed
Could be a mind alert to act just.
To care and refrain from those things oft concealed,
Even though the mass would control what they think must—
Be it the drive to achieve coins and paper.
What force of nature gives persons want for froth
Such as will to gain what seems of such taper
To illumine their stay on earth as a broth,
Stoking their gullets and proclaiming henceforth:
The measure of a great mind making it known
With show to be noticed by those with false fame.
Compare with those who act from great kindness grown
As restraint is to playing an errant game.
The soul is stirred from the spirit of goodness,
Achieved by the love of helping someone else—
To see another life lived in moral oneness,
To find with others shared joy with someone else.

That Day

That day, the afternoon sun shone through the leaves
Along sides of the street in short-sleeve weather.
Fronting the dormitory buildings was the wide lee's
Sheltered street where students crossed together.
Some with books standing talking, some without,
Free to enjoy the casual carefree time—
A life known then as moments all about
Being there in that cloistered setting sublime.
The smell of trees and fresh-cut grass glistening
In the reflections as gazing soft set
Peering eyes searched for thoughts of christening
Some relatable experience yet
To be discovered in that haze of life.

That day, mind pinioned motionless staring,
Looking across the street in eclipsed strife—
Conflict of time between moving, caring,
That perplexing lonely moment so clean,
Without that fixture linking to exist—
My sight suddenly struck clearly serene,
Someone crossing as if now I could persist
So my detached mind could return to then,
When my world needed inclusion to track
With the human quick-start to life again,
With a touch of warmth for what I did lack.

Grasping back to that date for renewal,
My memory becomes the mind and heart.
Those moments relived rest like a jewel,
Precious in time when God blessed a start
In a setting where young languor found truth
In the surroundings where my mind did wait,
And the freshness of love gave pause to youth.
That day gave my life time to relate.

As now, that day lives a wonderful mystery—
Those moments so succinct in history.
The green foliage is our wreathed memory
That caresses our hearts' long symmetry.
Our first street has sanctified our true way.
How blessed the time now lasted from that day.

Transitory Dilemma

Awakening from that mantle of pictures
That viscid time, which holds luxuriate
Reluctance to admit the real of day
To force itself with direct drawn strictures,
Penetrating eyes to infuriate
The visceral contact realm of dream delay;

Then rising to touch the unwelcome floor
To steady from a self-assault to balance
What was internally connectable
With the frames one must face as were before,
When one lived in a world without semblance
Of want to guide the unmanageable.

A Sanctuary

Unwilling to move the clutter of my fueled desk—
Magazines, envelopes, papers, stacks of unshelved books,
Subjects to be leafed to, to excite the mental engine
Would give to me where to go to contemplate a busy quest.
More than a surface to cogitate the games of battlement
    rooks—
But an enclosure to hold knowledge unimpaired and sanguine.

Not soundproof, for outside can be heard wafts of Christmas
    near,
So appropriate there resides the familiar and unknown—
Ideas and thoughts foraging from fingertips withdrawn.
Not from the dark dungeons of a thief hidden in fear,
But exposed to a seeking mind lurking to be self-flown
To find those thoughts between now and when once He did
    appear.

Catalogued wisdom past written to help us all live now.
The journey now is remaining years still able to yearn
Through a sanctuary where one is left so important
To gain interpretations where one may diligently plough.
The travel to outside is limited to one's will to learn.
Surface is long and wide, but deep the human compartment.

Winter's Look

The street is a black ice gray before the light of day.
Must be it rained last night but morning brings no spray—
Would be good to clean it that way.

Sunlight may not splay itself through and brighten the town,
depending on the place its bar beams can laser down—
corners of the buildings block its coming down.

Train on the tracks off scraping, sending a traveling sound.
At least one thing cleans—its frictional touch squeaks around.
Circles turn and vibrate off the railed ground.

Buildings and street lights radiate and moisture is dried.
Only a little, though many sources provide warmth to be plied
to restore heat when sources are tried.

Looking out my window, my floor temperature vent sends
    warm air.
My reluctant feet refuse to descend on the outside air
onto the street front to find the paper there.

Morning sounds blend with weather to predict the waking day.
Somehow the haunting cold is sighted in a breathed air way
that signals don't go out; stay.

It seems only the little birds flit from tree to tree
on winter's gnarled limbs remaining naked, no leaves to see—
some sparkle where leaves fail to be.

Magnetized by slim hope the day will clear for me to go,
but the early look does not authenticate my desire to grow—
willingness to enter winter's flow.

Soon the street will have its usual bumper crops of cars
humming by, plying the streets like longitudinal spars,
growing, as the day, in lines of responsive exemplars.

Now and then over the rooftops, through the dim distant light,
wait for the mountain projections, seen in their Olympian
     right,
as their snow-peaked cliffs overlook my plight.

My it's-early-yet attitude holds me finding other views.
If the morning paper is not extracted, what of the news,
but then what need to meet the street crews?

Sometimes there is such sense of control in my storied condo
     look.
Wonderful to wake so early from my telling timepiece book—
play like God and afford my time to look.

So much can be learned to perceive between here and there.
Portions of the seasons resonate with pieces of each year—
so much to know and be free from fear.

Live in a land with gifts to take time to see and think
to choose to observe, have God's grace without a blink,
to enjoy the day and see winter's link.

Just Find

Strange to find one house not like the other.
When they look alike, they are still not the same.
Still built the same, but one must look further.
It's not the structure, not the building frame.
Two trees stand side by side in the front yard.
The wind and rain touches both in seasons.
Even though the same height, the cold does not retard.
Why they are different still exists reasons.
When people talk, it's about they are odd.
One seems to stand out, the other does not.
One dresses not to stand out, one seems mod.
There are those who observe, conclude on the spot.
Growth is the key to be found quite mature.
One has changed and noticed to what degree.
Expression can be noticed to be sure.
To whom it's spoken may find they agree.
Most admire one person's eye for detail.
To see one's branches is not like the first.
Puts one to make a point not spoken to fail.
To show which mind has a cleverer burst.
In which case, a contest orders each day.
And the day must be using minds to win.
An exercise becomes what can be found to say.
And egos must reign when one must top again.
Differences exist and need not be blown.
The world needs not be always a test.
Separate is not a clever straight thrown.
It is not the way to grow at one's behest.
But to see the length and breadth of one's mind
Can be found from acceptance, and just find.

Living Promise

When days will reap my sense to feel
And art is what my mind will make;
And my thought will loose my heart's seal.
That calm, that trail, will track and take.

For my time is now, free to go
Beyond my life where I might stow
Away some bit, some nip to know
More than the rip and cut of curse,

To which I've come to stretch and turn—
Some new route, which will not be worse
That gives hope for newer concern
Drives me distances where I yearn.

But first questions I'm forced to ask
To have just books to read about
And picture arts to dream the task
To seek those I have need to tout.

Such a search must have a clear mark,
A point of aim, but just how wide?
The trip must be more than just a lark
Since now age has told me to abide.

So now time calls me to measure,
A regret not to be forsaken,
How distant can I seek my treasure.
A plan has become something taken.

But time allows things already gained,
As when moving, learn from the past.
Some important things have remained
So the newly attacked may last.

Cultures are out there to explore.
Places to search still can be found.
More ways to see may be in store,
Refinements from a different ground.

If God will let my sense to feel
And my mind the range of what's there,
Then books and arts will not conceal
What they reflect through life's free air

To see and hear and know the now
As it ties with the past in growth
Will surely give the way and how
To live and retain life's own oath.

In spite of place, color, or creed
How one lives the life God gave
Is most important to all indeed.
Such a promise we strive to save.

Viscose

A handicap of thought—
Like the use of Post-its,
To break the cellophane,
Tear away the viscose,
And etch what words have wrought.
Accept the use of the age.
"Master the circumstance,"
The known reverend said.
Books help my mind to think.
Put all the words to bed;
Awaken from new groups—
Find use in other ways.
Break into what is known
And spark with other days.
No vacuum gives ignition.
Life exists with attrition.
Accept not this condition.
The world of worth is full.
Travel to the mental brink.
Relate to the preconceived.
By virtue we can think.
Take each script *in virtu*—
Let it search the believed.

The Scripture does note,
"If you have ears to hear,"
Also the eyes to see.
Others write; others read,
Birds I see fly over—
They land and find a seed.
Veils cloud what we perceive.
Human minds have the power—
Like a bird they can go
With freedom to relieve.
Where life can give to look,
The heart can feel a book,

Or one who wrote the words.
So many words to see
And find their worth to us.
Promise and assurance
Pose what life can be.

I Streetlight

There is the power to stimulate sight.
My condition of the space so present,
Delineates the bright from the shadow.
So often it is thought the wrong from the right.
It is clarified when made incandescent.
Such imminence portrays a strange credo.
Symbols are not actual, not strict light.
Down from my metallic habit wimple,
Through my glass protected face I shine
Into the vestiges of closed night.
To those who look up, I look quite simple.
My light is radiated, not divine,
With steady spark serving just to ignite.
My one aspect is in giving regard.
Great words describe me beyond my flash source.
Sometimes used metaphors like alert
And enlightenment by some reaching bard—
Even related to mental, of course.
But electromagnetic wavelength, my only concert.

Common Small

How small to say molecular is not common small.
Use of the words "tiny" and "little" lends not wise help.
Comparing the big picture to measure wherewithal,
The size or shape is like the ocean to so much kelp.

Where, oh, where can be found the right word to say best—
The sight of a flower nestled so cozily to see,
Single description must be taken from noting the rest.
Such delicate charm pervades what surrounds it to be.

Yet, each one of us is unique among all the rest.
To grow and thrive with some personal road to one's quest
Does not make need for creating some profounding test,
Unless people must have oneness known at their behest.

Conjecture

Snaillike movements are not instantly perceptible.
Naked clear sheet so natural in its free cover,
With days periodically closing over us all.
Unfailing in all climes, humans spin unpredictable;
But most do not wait to give truth of its earth hover.
Only attention is drawn from its replacement call—
When it can no longer cease its forestall.

With a smooth phoenix rise each time by daily course,
We waken for what business is placed its due,
Since the command controls, for all plants our living force,
We depend our lives all days, until its light is through,
On what clarity given from its momentous implants.
It is a gift regarded often as happenstance.

Then comes a morbid net, sinking on every surface.
So slowly it comes that eyes must adjust their focus.
And artificial rays try to extend framed days—
Human ingenuity claims time for each new artifice.
Reception is deemed so needed in every locus,
Natural earthly day must wane again from the crocus.
New expectations come through the darkening nightfall.
Less seen are winds of chance, which sweep and stray effects
So evenings descend to conclude each daylight's test
With different views to be relegated to all.
The night for some means time slows when evening reflects.
Life's periodic surcease comes to await and rest.
Day and night exceed the other's delay to contest.

Whether times are humanly foretold predilections,
Whether preferences come from each scheme or desire,
The natural patterns will come and go no matter what.
No matter what relationships bring, what afflictions,
Living results in the known or what unknowns transpire.
Human living does coincide God's wonders with plot—
Find the given use of day and night, surmise or not.

Convolution

In the warm crib, living through newborn days,
Waiting until the mobile life arrives
May stand and hold, hopes in all ways
To examine other lives.

The homeful house, spacing enough where to go,
Provides a protective world, free enclosure
Where soft comfort, tailored to easy flow—
A place for composure.

In the serial open streets found clearly marked,
Pointing in many directions, sorted for each mind,
Travel must be planned before leaving is embarked
To move and find.

Congregate in cities with codes and rules,
Securing the father's restraints, more rapid pace,
Cautions to be taken, enforcing by machines and fools,
To keep it a safe place.

Countries far away, traveling with visas and passports,
Differing languages, and culture traits,
Obtaining proof of separation, how one comports,
To suggest how one rates.

Degrees of isolation, existing restraints
Are there through guises of aspiration.
The facts of human conditions, engulfing territorial
      complaints,
Human dignity needs restoration.

The child becomes with a sense of self and love,
Fostered in the world, seeing and feeling respect,
Where mistakes and growth are reprieved from above,
Refrain temerities for human effect.

Discovery

The sun is coming through, making shadows in the hall,
A testimony to man's need to give the light a chance.
So would I be the man to find more than Hadrian's wall;
Conquer not forceful fame but open words to romance.
Reach out from within the heart, illumine distant shores.
To be seen must come from what senses may touch the soul.
The mise-en-scenes reflect more than what comes through the
    pores,
Than what study absorbs from one celestial pole.
Ulyssean wanderings will not depict the way,
Each truth must be sought wherever the heart will find itself.
Traverse forth in quest of each truth; my heart will not stray.
A whale slips through until reaching each watery shelf.
What will sustain is an appetite for what others know.
The deep and small knowledge gives mysterious details,
For life is more than mere patterns of respite then flow.
It cannot be a matter when search ultimately fails—
All journeys can reunite with a porous common good.
All hearts who seek receive the inner joys of small things.
Each mental plunge succeeds where life can be understood.
The soul is not limited to what discovery brings.

Inference

The wink.
A parted chasm brooked the light
On a smooth facial appurtenance,
With no intentional wrinkle
Below, between mouth or chin.
Yet deep within a twinkle
Rushed as if to give in.
But no sign came outright,
Save a guess one might make.
Careful not to trip and fall
Into a seductive crypt—
Deep notions slip the void
When can't be seen a wall.
Sensual torment.

Presence

Dollops of white weave as a part—
Genetic or nature's art,
Thick and combed prominent contrasts.
Continuing beauty lasts.
Once she had lighter blond to start,
Now kind years have blessed her heart,
And symbols of wisdom's gentle flair
Make young lives want to turn to her—
None forgotten her soft spirit
When in places see her again,
Flowing strands, remember her then.
Now turn to sweetness always been
And gain presence from her company.

Nature Can Tell

The light kept streaming from a cloudless sky.
Traffic moved without hesitation.
Landscapes in all their clarity passed by.
As often happens comes speculation—
A mind drifting from things unresolved—
People problems betwixt a pastoral scene—
Feelings invading concerned involvement—
Mind-bending trips trying not to careen.
Still the heart keeps the pace, distraction fires
Lick away at the kindling sticks burning.
Human living is a complex of desires.
Success finds answers to controlling yearning.
The warm earth receives the sun's healing rays.
Multiple of sounds fade into sameness—
A melding of sounds no longer betrays
Any sense of man and vehicle oneness.
Farms and pasture lands fuse tranquility.
Musings of time ease lingering conflicts—
One grows tired testing one's ability.
Open spaces displace so many layered sticks.
Then, from the houses down to the fields to fences,
There, on a post, was stationed a little hawk.
Thinking it was strange captured the senses.
Pieces of thinking sidetracked to gawk
At a bird of prey between farm and highway.
Quickly by came another post-preying bird.
Soon it was more posted birds that one day.
Why did this happening seem so absurd?
Was it a time field mice were plentiful,
Or small creature game so available?

To wonder about these birds diurnal,
And observe these instances debatable,
And to question their authenticity
Made the observer seem insatiable
To conjure quite an eccentricity
To relieve quite a contentious congestion.
But his troubled thinking meshed so well
That from that day he reasoned an obsession—
Divert to more pleasant things and dispel
People problems from what nature can tell.

The Fray

Favor the light that provokes the day.
Extend into the night the frame
That serves as respite for the fray.
The minstrel clowns to entertain
For all who can have sense to gain.
Like flowers appear to give attraction,
Bloom and bring out their color bain
To serve and flaunt their distraction
And take their strength from the pain.

The water runs through days and nights
And cuts through the canyons it makes.
The sun's heat melts the snow for flights
Of rippling torrents from fusioned flakes.
It dances over rocks and weaves its way
Down to the streams, rivers and the sea.
Mankind must trap and make it stay
Within the confines of submission be.

Depend we must for nature's sustenance.
The earth is owned by those who cry the best.
Those who don't must suffer their penitence,
Or satirize the great to make a test.
The streets and roads connect the space.
Journeys are made from low to high,
And life is endured by winning the race.
Up or down is gained by those who intensify.

Transducers become the makers of things.
Resources exist when controlling the find.
Humans will gain from what discovery brings,
Therefore governing by influencing mankind.
Towers of wealth dole out for the many—
The mice, the moles provide the food,
Whether the wage be dollar or penurious penny.
Will the march for gain not others exclude?

Devices to speak compute the power.
Our own ingenuity informs us.
Mogul might procures the lucred tower
And dispenses like the Creator Spiritus,
And like the rain, quench the persevered thirst.
Under the sky atop the human heap
But raised to spread means of energy's burst,
Competition controls electrode creep.

From the opened chrysalis of life
A quiescent pore offers its exposure.
The strain begins being posed for strife—
Inflictive tumult of sense disclosure,
And youth are taught to take the upward leap.
Fain the impractical quixotic surge.
Prepare to control youth's buoyant splurge;
Prepare to guard against self-surging defeat,
And work time to meter a wasteful urge.

The seeking to reach that *sub voce* success,
Where growth proceeds with society's toll,
One grasp through stages maintaining the stress.
Many break through values that others extol.
Somewhere in this sustained terminate road,
Somewhere in this ingrain for ambit worth
Human feelings reside, will not corrode,
And fellow souls will find goodness on earth.

Endure

What is this on my face I feel?
The buildings seem the same to me;
The evening comes and pierces me.
Almost as if a foreign breath will peel.
Do they also suffer naked?
Some metal, some wood-layed siding—
Little protection always there abiding.
Where they lap the cold invaded.
Not enough clothes to hug the skin;
The steady dent dry wipes the flesh.
The pores take it like molded mesh.
Constant it lays, will not say when.
I walk, it does not do the same.
It seeps with silent speed intense,
Though unseen it gives no pretense.
Look around no clue where it came.
My eyes and ears must take the drink,
Must absorb the sly even flow.
Until I push through it does know
I reach a place, then cold will shrink.

Enveloped

Capture the Promethean leaks through the leaves.
Movement underneath breaks the streaks of dazzling glares.
Patterns flicker down walking amidst the trees,
Slashing between dark blotches now become flares—
Tenuous beauty finds seeping nature's wares.
Shards on the ground solace what would be a shadow
And open the soul to multilayered flashes.
Light through the trees marks a glorious meadow
Fed by a nearby brook the grass there stashes
The moisture gleaming in strips softly endow
Light and shadow's visible, temporary art.
Something of the divine comes down to this place.
Shall we not rationalize God's grace to start
Our heart's bliss to receive this, His common trace?
His symbol so wonderful rare to replace,
But to stop and be enveloped in His grace.

Warless Defense

The dump trucks clanged dropping small rocks of coal
Between the barrack rows and the Orderly Room.
Snow covering the yard contrasted with each troll
Shovel of blackish chunks, to fire a smoke plume,
Were seldom wheelbarrowed to a furnace.
Bitter weeks passed by when John L's miners struck.
Cold mornings scoured sore-rubbed skin from pumice,
Either cold sponge clean baths or be out of luck.
It was windy marching to mechanic's school.
Nor was our barracks warm spots on our return.
Greasy coveralls each day became the rule.
The Union worker's strike was our worn concern.
Living through those times tested each youth's mettle.
Soldiers were subject to peacetime politics.
Warless defense paused for workers to settle.
Lessons were learned without word conflicts.

Regium Donum

Filling the air, gathering the slow roaming crescendos,
Enriching in their particulates of amassing sound,
My heart warms as my mind swirls in silent innuendos.
Nothing disturbs the perfect atmosphere, feelings abound,
And I think of pleasant but surreal mysteries around.
Life as I know it departs with the rising freeing grace,
As the voices blend with the sweet music's deepening trace.
I'm almost annoyed by no longer quiet exhalations
That cause me to find breathing for noisy obligations
The conflict between breathing and glorious expectations.
Latin words, amalgamated sounds, I can't interpret;
But no matter, the lightness and depthness ease my surfeit,
The aches and pains of my conscious do ease away.
My soul is lifted from the surly smog of disarray,
And the composer's mind wafts into my own sense display.
Wanderings of the daily turmoils, some fancy, some real,
Tortured struggles of conscious myths, dreams my mind will
        conceal,
Are pushed behind with a fresh spirit I can longer feel.
Awakening the harmonic impact on me to a place—
A place that gives me strength though I were indominable.
Moments in time relieve my flashbacks' clinging embrace.
Now, long as the symphonic sound lasts, soars formidable,
So pervades my heart to show its livened freeing grace;
Though I wish it would last, I have been flown above the cruel
        race.
It must be—it has to be a gift when souls find a need—
A need to be lifted up to know beyond human greed—
A meditation melding of heart and music to exceed.

Direction

Life breaks in on our eyelids—
Sweet breath of another day
Woos to clear some intrepid's
Way yet unseen to display
In gold sheen to strike the eyes
And fume the heart so heroic,
From our dream states made stoic,
By meanings not intended
When feeling and words blended.
Promise, please, bring life today
Unsullied by bent delay,
Received words misunderstand
When thrust hurts a pent-up heart
And cause a will to take command
And lead away from the start.

Give direction, direction.
Let my soul not weigh more hearts.
Let me cause not affliction
By some phrase from me departs.
May portals freely open,
Words used kindly spoken.
No test be made for safe intent
But kindness be always meant.
What more important the day
Than to strive for that which may
Be just good union further,
And make attachment to another
Belong to every soul.
Housing is often defaced.
All eternal from pole to pole.
Enter all words gently placed.

Center of Things

A memory foregone is a consciousness lost.
To memorize the day prohibits a mind tossed,
And secures a life's journey prospected ahead—
Where one knows having been steers surer roads instead.
So pay attention to the rewards of the day.
Suffer the fusion of an experience delay,
While moving in the now of each action indeed;
A life is lived and generation will proceed.
An art is performed through each interactional move.
Human to human, life to life is all to prove.
The world habitation creates by choice and selects—
Together finds all forms of fusible prospects.
Two humans compose the precise center of things—
Things of supply, of growth from what all movement springs.
Miracles are contacts between all that's wondrous,
And the work of love succeeds through all that's ponderous.

II

A KING'S ELEGANCE

The eternal being . . . as it lives in us, also lives in every animal.

—Arthur Schopenhauer, *Essays*

We Both Did See

Up the winding forest trail I went,
Went not caring the time I spent.
The start was new; the day was clear,
Was keen to solve some body fear.
A search was made to find just how
Was best for me to find right now
Just what my strength would stand to take
For the journey up I wished to make.
Along the way it came to me
There were things for me to see.
Foremost were trees so green and tall,
Stood straight, erect to cover all.
On one great tree high on a limb
Just by a bend from a rock rim—
From there looked up—there he was!
There an eagle, just perched he was!
Perched there ready to fly away.
Stood there to see him—"Don't fly away,"
I thought with surprise what to say.
Then asked of him, "Please, won't you stay?"
Not knowing now what else he will;
But did not move—we both stood still.
And then he flew up, out of sight.
First I felt sad I made him go,
A being so free—there too was he.
But I—I came and touched his tree.
Could not know that this would scare him.
Then, as I walked around the rim,
He soared as did I, this earthly thing,
Then this other waved just at me.
He knew somehow we both did see.

Protect His Stillness

Standing there on the post seemed without a notion
Which way to go that would make a graceful motion.
Wonder absorbs a mind that sees him stand
Like a picture with now and again the wind
Raising feathers so gently disturbing the grand
And picturesque stillness so stately to defend.
One seeks, upon seeing, to gain a closer look
At this momentary creature so still from his flight.
Many paint his blank image to put in a book,
But no page gives all truth to such a placid sight.
His controlled freedom allows him to be
In his resting solitude for us to see.
Such a contrast from graceful glides in the air
When he turns into the breeze and slides along,
Seems not caring to move so close to stare.
It may be he came to stop here to avoid the throng,
Or protect our chance for his brief appearance,
And give him a moment to take his turn
On the post before away to go into his disappearance.
Not too close will somehow let him learn
That again when that post is unoccupied and free
And another brethren is off to see what he will see
In our minds will last a pleasant memory.

Searching Pass

At breakfast one morning came an instant decision.
What caused it all was a most pulling sight.
Mid-air fingering of my coffee cup locked in position,
Afraid he might bolt away in sudden fright,
That we froze with a fixed stare at this momentary feature.
Outside, top of our rugged hypericum covered bank he stood—
This frail brownish and gray four-legged creature
A moment stopped nose down, searching for what he could,
And never turned to notice us watching him through the glass.
So curiously we wondered what it was caused him to stop—
Eagerly wishing him to stay longer in his somewhat searching
     pass.
Startling opportunity it was for us to see him atop
Our small world, sharing himself when we both started our
     day.
Wherever he strolled this was his traveled space.
We could imagine that he found this locale to stray
Away from some area more suited to his comfort and place.
But what a blight of smugness that belief would be!
Wasn't he entitled to go where he might find,
And search for everything he would need to see?
Who were we to restrict his track and see him as a different
     kind?
That morning we shall not let ourselves forget
We were, through our window, witnessing an interesting other,
And we will always remember and never be beset
By the blockages that hinder us from seeing further.
He did not need to see us stealing a glimpse of his position,
For he had stopped for a moment to sense his decision.
We happened to be there where he paused to ponder.
We happened to be there where we paused to wonder.

World View

What in the world is meant by a "World View?"
Still better, whose world is being suggested?
Every day one decides for oneself what is true;
But continues to be pushed to take it digested,
As if the road to awareness is a single look for everyone—
That to be humanly alert, all under the sun
That experiencing from all contingencies can be done.

Heard about the Makahs harpooning a whale.
Pictures were taken of sticking this fishlike marine.
An old tradition was celebrated, and they would not fail
To heist the carcass, ending a life serene,
Producing for all the tribe to cut, tear, and taste—
Acknowledgment to the world a proper rite
At the expense of a mammal removed from sight.

What is the effect on all who would see
This ceremonial killing of a mammal roaming free?

Conversational Meddler

If asked about your domesticated carnivore,
You could answer "Don't have one."
Of course, this protruder might need to pry more,
In which case, maybe it's all in fun
To pose an inquiry about a flesh-eating mammal.
That, to say the least, is, in a simple word, tame.
You would think, "Ah, this boob is playing a game!"
Then you could answer, "What mammal?"
And venturing further to show him up, could say,
"My dog is a vertebrate fed on milk."
And then to play the verbal game, by reason of causing dismay,
"He is different from the rest of his ilk."
Now which would be touting some zoological propensity?
Each then would be just another intellectual buttinsky.

Little Fur Piece

Through a tunnel of diminished light—
There at the end is a focused object,
A square frame that draws your sight
And causes closer observation of its subject.
A young Amish girl out of a shadow
Holding on her shoulder a kitten,
Grasped in comfort with her love to endow
This little fur piece nestled like a mitten
With her fingers enmeshed in its fur,
Looking away from the front of a shed.
Her eyes appear forlorn that nothing will occur—
A moment of loneliness feeling to be fed.
Both sightless dream and tender touch
Suggest that there was a time gone passed,
When the sense of love was not so much,
Was only thought about but did not last.

Bushtit

The traffic was heavy into the bush.
From different directions they seemed to come.
One shrub seemed more thick and lush,
Providing a disappearing end of a journey from
What distance none of us could fathom.
Small little creatures they were,
With amazing speed they fluttered in.
Hummingbirdlike in size and sphere,
Each came scurrying again and again,
One by one touching leaves in airy spasm.
They found their place to enter.
We kept our eyes to not one entrance,
But focused a long time on the center
Of the place that each observed in a trance.
Some moved closer to find just one
Sitting or standing on a tightly packed limb.
(If one could be found landed from the run.)
We all thought they found a perch, but slim
It would have to be for each a place to hide.
We looked but none found one in or out
Of the place they went, we guessed, to abide.
Strange tiny wingers! From where did they fly?
And this place! To where did they go?

Soon tiring of sighting, the scene did mystify.
No answers could we find to know.
So small and so quick we remarked,
But no conclusion came to our query.
The discussion faded on where they embarked.
All surmised nature concealed its own theory.

A King's Elegance

A search in the bush where once were tall trees,
Now are made short for their tops must comply,
We rode through crowded space under a searing sky.
And over dirt, white bleached for one who sees
Ahead, bumpy with animal prints honest and dry
In a day where no wind was out of place,
Along a narrow curved road where branches scrape loose
On the rover's sides, one must lower the head and face,
And there to see quickly away scurries a startled mongoose.

A primitive difference no human nostril scent did pierce
But from the odors of a machine that bounced us around
With strained sounds snarl and choke astride the ground.

Finally, what passed for a road opened out at the end,
And a humming sound bounded on to a new landscape
Of open dirt, which held no bush as its friend.
Under and around tires lay clumps of similar shape.
All eyes looked at what the depositors had given.
And then we noticed between the open sky and dirt,
Off in the distance in the direction we were driven,
A grand prize lurched forward not yet coming alert
To this rumbling object encroaching from behind.
Could this large creature be unimpressed by our kind?

To look too hard and too long is an insulting state.
To things so large and so different is an invasion.
When value of concentration is an admirable trait,
To interrupt another's travel induces a repugnant sensation.
When the power of the machine moved to his course,
We blocked his path, an irritant to this king.
Yet noticing this intrusion, he did not use force,
But went a farther way, away from the thing
That he wished to find, allowing our insistence
To deter his direction by accepting our persistence.

124

His grace and massive size as we passed by,
Ignoring our calloused and ignorant endeavor,
Displayed an example of elegance and stability for all of us to
    try—
A lesson to be learned when thought we were so clever.

Holding Plea

Morning views are allowed earlier when closer to the sky.
The clearing light pierced my eyes but so gently why
Wondered my mind when no-longer sleep would comply.

The urge fought the signal to wake and rise to see,
But sleep was not ready to succumb to a day's view;
So time was taken for comfort's holding plea.

My air was cool that needed the sun's reflective desire,
And a glance around the Lookout demanded my vigil
To be done for forest's protection from destructive fire.

So I thought in my delirium between night and day
As I blinked to be raised to the smells of May,
And the pull of dawn to look without delay.

On my elbows I rose to glimpse through my glass,
Peering out from my high place, there a grand thing
Raised its solemn nose, a close surprising trespass.

Startled I was afraid to move and held my mind
As his white-horned head raised, our eyes met.
All previous thought stood still for another kind.

He stared as did I, wondering what next to do.
One must move and neither seemed all through—
Me of my wakened sleep; he if his sight were true.

Suddenly, he moved and gently stepped from sight.
I raised to see him go; but as he came, I guessed, so he went
Silently, effortlessly to another place to alight

Again upon another mount to take a positional point
With nothing to stare at and disturb his higher perch.
His sovereign being could gain another place to anoint.

It Was Time

That morning I looked—
Still in his box with sad eyes.
The garage door left open,
Letting the morning light in
With the smell of a clear fresh day
And mowed grass still lingering
Untouched by his once vigorous feet.
But he couldn't raise himself.
Tried to give him some hamburger meat.
He loved hamburger meat.
His love and taste mixed in his heart—
Weakly he smelled but couldn't.
Had to lift his body out,
Brown, black and silver-tipped.
No need to have his great collar.
Saved his life once
When another's teeth wouldn't enter.
God would take him without neck piece.
Heavy into the seat beside me
He breathed a little chirp of pain.
No one but me would take him.
When my daughter was questioned once,
She answered, "He's my brother."
Turned into the vet's drive early.
Sat beside him as he lay on his side,
Paw and eyes touched,
The last time in the car.
Finally, carried him inside,
Waited on the floor in back,
Preparations were being made.
Lay down beside him
My hand on his noble back.
Then it was time.
On the table his eyes showed no fear.
Gently given, one breath and gone—
Life went out; I drove home alone.

Where

Dashing around the outgrown roots,
Climb here, he decided, this one here.
This one's nice trunk, have no fear—
No need to look, dart by shoots,
Little green ones, tickled his rear.

A place to romp, jump and stray
To see the sights, feel the sun,
Pick the way up, choose the run—
His special tree, this branch today,
This tree, that branch for him to play.

So fast he went, climbing quickly by.
Even the bumpy bark, a paw-hold
To ease the sprint, up and bold,
He whisked himself toward the sky
To reach his place, one more try.

Then suddenly, a bark-gripped stop—
No farther up, he could not reach.
The trunk—gone—that was on top.
Nothing, not a crack or possible breach
He could undergo, not a paw-held drop.

From side to side he glanced about.
He held tighter, now no place to know,
But this way up, a familiar route
He always rummaged; he could always go
There to trip and move so far out.

His tail now twitched a peculiar way,
Not up or down or sideways flick.
Where could he go? No movement quick
Could clear his mind this unknown way.
He could not believe this disarray.

Then a tree-trimmer saw him there,
Hugging the bark, staring into the air.
He said to himself, "Little guy is lost."
He clapped his hands for a little scare.
Jumping circular as if he were tossed,
Speeding down, tail up, to ground, crossed,
Off away he scurried to who knows where.

There was a tree, a favorite place
That no longer is, not a trace.
Our little friend played, where he chose.
Don't see him now, miss his flight
Onto the branches, streaking he rose—
Then down he went, following his nose,
Only to retreat away, out of sight.

Gravitas

He walks across his held ground with singular grace,
Steps forward with alert presence to a specific place.
Little energy is lost in control of his massive means,
As he marches with steady pace to clear useful scenes
That can give his imposing carriage surcease of the day.
Where he walks nothing is so binding as to deter his way.
Although he prefers uncluttered space to make his walk,
His oval-shaped roundness makes him obvious to stalk
For those impressed to pour back an astonished glance.
Nature provided great protuberances not by chance—
A noble trunk, lengthy tusks, precede his upright advance.
They lead him as he holds them high and pointed free
To make way should any encumbrances chance to be.
No effrontery shall block his path or restrict his need
To reach the glorious pool in which he may submerge,
And rinse his audacious presence and satiate his urge.
Some may say, who have the gall to exclaim his size,
As huge and ungainly and immeasurable, may give rise
To their own world view, assumed sightfully proportionate.
But his proper shape for his wants are indeed fortunate.
His largesse has no case to rise above or kowtow to.
His life is unashamed and unabashed. Most may construe
That where he lives is not appropriate or within his grasp.
He has no need or inclination to expound such contrast.
His size, his place is of no concern for other's observance,
For his value, his worth recognizes no social disturbance.

Wait and Stare

He had to wait and stare
In the cold, damp air,
For someone to come back,
For someone who must lack
Any caring for his ordeal,
To think how he did feel.
People passed, he did not care,
He just had to wait and stare.
His lean body looked very grim—
Shivering legs, mere sticks for him,
Standing there on frozen pavement,
Couldn't sit in this enslavement.
A post was there to hold him.
Seemed he was just as slim.
To a scrag of rope he was tied,
Couldn't move about if he tried,
Looked rough around his neck,
Made him look like a speck
Among those who passed by.
Most ignored; none asked why.

Somewhere we must hope to find
That all life needs to be kind.
Here was a conscious dog,
Treated as if he were a mindless log
To step around, be in the way—
Could he speak, what would he say?

That Morning's Release

His time was waiting.
Sprawling by the patio doors,
Through the glass,
grizzled chin on his paws,
observing what moved.
It was his door
to the outside world.
It was his place
to lie in the sunshine.
He almost knew
when to pay his dues.
His always patience
he had learned,
living inside the house.
Early morning was his
to be leashed
to search outside
through the weedy grass
and up the bank
behind,
through the trees.
That morning
I clipped into his collar,
opened the sliding door
to the pull of fragrant smells.
Releasing the triggered reel,
up the rocked bank
we both grappled,
him on churning fours,
me with leaping twos.
Something distracted!
He lunged so hard
he broke the cord.
Into the trees
he flew.
Never had I seen
such ferocious scramble.

"Max!" "Wait!"
Something drew him
away from me
into his instinctual world.
(The moment,
sometimes,
so magnetic,
demands release.)
Around the trees
I found him
standing over
a tiny gray squirrel,
splayed on the ground,
body heaving,
eyes wide in fear.
Grabbing Max,
I hurried us away,
down the bank,
into the house.
Closing him in,
I returned
to assist;
but he was gone.

A Way Out

Gliding, he comes in on the thermal air,
Through the open end from the lake, his flare.
Above and around the field he dips down;
Then back up he soars the stadium crown,
Searching, wandering the tumultuous sound.
He seems a clear white moment, so bound;
Now is he dispatched to a wayward spree—
Bearings lost, a distraction, this melee?
Unused to this crowd congested below—
Circular fracas grants no place to go.
We came to watch scuffling bodies compete,
Cheers for helmets cracking, destining defeat,
Youthful armies, striking physical feat!
But there is the void of space swinging through
This seeming wistful winged wayfarer came too!
Once sliding the air over calm waters,
Unconfined, free, with other self-starters,
He has found himself wanting a way out.

Debauchery

We were all looking but could see none.
The road was rough and the dust clouded up.
Our range rover hobbled road rhythm
So that the sky lurched into the sun.
Sprinting off to the side could not interrupt
A mongoose, like an heraldic emblem,
Slithered in a prehistoric run.
Chewed tree tops left limb sticks poking out
Dry and leafless vibrating fiddles,
Plucking sound as we knocked by.
By a dry lake bed festering about
Two carcasses, foul birds picked middles,
Parts decayed matter drying in a sty.
Two young starving lions hid in the bush.
To eat, to eat when such waste was left
In this arid land where animals live
And move to devour in hunger's rush
Did not allow sight those who were bereft,
Was not the place the terrain could give
Us what we looked for and would see none.

Passing Plateau

We climbed the bucked-out trail.
The sun was high, the sky clear,
And our pack horse would not fail
His sure clumping hooves. I, in rear,
Followed fellow climber front,
Making the three sometimes strain
The long hike day, though errant
At times, finding markers' gain
To be sure we knew to go
From the old range to the new.
Hoping soon to make the slow
Journey inward to a slew,
A position change, a slope
Rising up the side, steep mountain
Wall onto a precipice,
A rising narrow fountain,
Or jetting waterfall hiss
Up ahead around the path.
Under the slippery fall,
Cooling from the hot sun's wrath
For a moment refreshed our stall,
And then through the other side.
Over a slight little rise,
We slowed in broken stride
For an extended plateau,
Widened flat jutting out
Over rocks supporting below.
Easing down our curved route,
We made for noon camp, a fire,
Resting ourselves and our horse,
Cooked beans and bacon, a source
With our map found our desire
To take some time. (This canyon
Would give radiant sight.)
For miles we and companion
Soared our eyes a mystic rite,

Not knowing centuries before
In the Pleistocene time,
More than temperature lore,
What glacial fluctuations
Made the Quaternary epoch.
Evidence the ice did sever
Deep into the chasmic rock.
(Now miles runs a flowing river;
Life's sustenance we could have
And all new creatures therein.)
Soon our rest was like a salve.
With consoled strain came a din.
Turning with a start first came
A deer loping toward our camp.
Stopping short, above us lame;
One leg drawn up like a cramp,
Unevenly passed into the woods.
Surprised, unable to stand
(Except our horse already stood)
A growling sound soon followed.
The same almost abrupt stop
Braced a bear. Tongue not swallowed,
Hanging out in a snorting flop,
He paused to make up his mind.
We and our horse could not move.
He, unfazed, galloped on to find
This instant not to intrude,
Passed on uninterrupted.

Zealous Burst

Crowds of lives come and go.
Stand off or go with them
is a choice in life to make.
Flights of ducks slide and flow
over the water, closely skim
the surface and rise to take
the air to find the wind.
But they follow a leader,
who soars on their slip stream
in some instinctual blend.
This individual feeder
being followed as if his dream
will sustain all who fly
in unity with his search.
Yet who wants to fly first,
and who will not comply,
and seek not to besmirch
those in their zealous burst?

Again Touch the Sky

The clear morning light found not the inner wall.
Inside the deck was left in partial darkness,
Yet untouched by the early sun's rays, did not fall
Into the corners where there stayed starkness.
Moving one's eyes lower from the horizon line,
There was the hidden shelter for its rest.
How surprising to notice his restless sign,
Hesitant breathing caused me to halt to test
Whether to go closer and see more clearly
If he could be helped out of his distress.
This little sparrow had stopped by wearily
On my jutting deck, hiding from some duress,
For regained strength to again touch the sky.
What could I do to give his stay some relief
From whatever cause placed him so poorly awry?
Some torn bread crumbs, I thought, would comfort his brief
Respite from this displacement in my company.
Away to my kitchen, crumble some light bread,
Return to serve my guest, kindness accompany.
But now found he was gone. My presence instead
Gave him the new fear or strength to find the light.
What gave this tiny brain the will to seek flight?

Free to Fly

The nest, resting high where two limbs did converge,
Sits empty to all who would look up that time of day.
(The pro had said an eagle had been seen bringing food.)
It would not be seen unless one noticed the merge—
And upon seeing the somewhat circular wad would conclude
Two huge branches from a tall and large-trunked tree
Hold in perfect balance where a little eaglet must stay,
Until the parent returns from soaring in the air free,
Searching for food to feed the little one who could not yet fly.

Playing golf the day I looked up and spotted the nest,
I could not stay long enough to wait for the mother's return.
It would have been good if I could have paused for a rest
And think more about the mud, leaf, and twig home.
It would not escape my mind, though I did not try
Because I yearned to be there hence when it would learn
To use its wings and I could see it on its way to roam
The sky and find that same mother's freedom to fly.

I thought about the human education that I had had.
It's called formal from the time it starts. When I was a lad,
My mother took me from the breakfast table to school.
She let me be taught by others, as is the human way.
From those first days till now, like thread from a spool,
Education was artificially taught and I learned to read.
Both pain and joy came from knowing what to say,
The things I could and could not and things I must not—
All to find from teachers and books, right there, on the spot.
When I, one day much later might learn to soar on my own
To make it through the world where I could learn from others.

As I thought, being careful to notice where the ball had flown,
Made me envy all the little eaglets who must wait for their
    mothers.
And then, in a shorter time, contact the world they must find
    so real,
In which to them it would become so open with nothing to
    conceal.

Life Versus Domain

We named him Cyrano, though his nose was not long.
He was little but he could move with quickness and grace.
He had a way of twisting when in a peopled throng
His head would rise high, showing his round eyes and clear
    face.

When he chose to dart, he shone in his tuxedo coat,
His stopping and cutting always had precise intent;
And when he ran full-out, he seemed as if to float—
For he could cover ground to wherever his mind was bent.

We lived in a great three-story Antebellum home.
Surrounding the home was an encircling grassed yard
He considered his own, which gave him a place to roam
And check the planted flowers and shrubs to be on guard.

He knew the terrain and all who lived and hid there.
Times a rabbit would venture across with deft to spare.
It was a sight to see his full-speed chase through the air;
Though never did he catch, not once, this elusive hare.

Birds were also his treat to chase, while away his day,
Bark at creatures who might wish to invade his domain.
Not mighty in stature but swift of foot made his stay
In this realm of his life a perfect space to lay claim.

One day he found his match in kingness and grace.
With strangeness and bristle, a mammal that day did pass.
Such thing before he had not seen cross his chosen space.
He could not allow such ugliness go without class.

Using his quick cut to claw by, he fast flew around.
A wide circle breached him the scope to see and miss;
More circle turns made did not cause this pig give his ground.
On across he went, this new order, nothing came amiss.

In this world there are those who own and those who do not.
Space can be given save pride and willingness to give,
But into each life come the wise to hold the shot;
Allow others access to make ways to where they live.

Roadside Fox

Saw roadside one come through the grass at the side.
His pie-shape face and ears first came into view,
Avoiding a car he just changed his stride,
Then leaping to race to catch his prey anew.
Springing across from the roadside ditch's crest,
A piece of fur almost sideways slipped
Across the road with a prance he pressed,
But a car stopped this little bird being gripped
By a stretching little fox's hungry bite.

The Uncertain Cage

See him standing there, looking at you.
His body is erect; what does he see?
So poised he stands alert, from his view,
Who you are and he seems to know who you will be.
What he sees now, he thinks that is true.

Something there is found to stop and stare
When all he did before was find a gait,
But now he has come still to look there
At you, and now you think what made him wait
To freeze his stance and reach through air.

His stillness, so abrupt, what he thinks—
You are not the examiner, he is.
Who is outside; who is inside, time shrinks.
The time has come and when you cease to quiz,
Who is there or who exists; who blinks?

All live in a cage, but who made it?
And who studied the other in this world?
Progress between what is so close knit—
An instant despite all unfurled,
A moment of thought is real until split.

Waking to Crucial Departures

Waking in the cold crisp morning before daylight,
Knowing you must slough off the Army blanket tight,
One can look to the sun's seeping through windowed sight
Of miles of trails and trees leading to peaks snow bright.
In the distant mountains, standing with kingly crowns,
As if they must be guards of soldiery glory.
And now the branched-tipped icings like minstrel clowns
With sparkling hats appear old, long in venue, hoary.
For I soon must rise up from my bed, see them full,
And measure their safety from any fire-smoked line
That would make its way into my spy glass to pull
Me to triangulate with a princely incline
To precisely position on my Fire Finder.

Breaking the morning feel and stretching to morning's glare,
My first glimpse causes my blink to the sun's blinder.
As I adjust to the remaining cold night air,
Gradual heat will come as I glimpse directions;
Most around through encircling windows what will come.
Who knows what has happened since last sight's detections?
Three sides have distant points where my view must be from.
A fourth provides a trail back to my garbage pit.

Amid the increasing day, breakfast done,
A glance behind, from my little table where I sit,
There ferociously flailing, paws pulling, a run
Like motion is made through disposed cans and food.
A huge brown girth touching the edge of my waste hole
With front claws spinning and throwing, in his etude.
This denizen redistributed the landscape!
When finishing with his pernicious perusal,
Slowly he padded from his voracious rape,
And none were there to express any prompt refusal.

While certain magnificences exist for all,
More important things may exceed scenic grandeurs.
Life's needs when crucial depart from what may enthrall,
When the domain gives no matter where life meanders.

Not So Far

(A brief little message from two cats, Amos and Tuck)

My brother is gone, but not so far.
He'll be one other waiting star.
I got to meet him, but not so far.
Where he'll be, others there are.

It's never good to leave just now.
Loved ones must stay the present way.
They'll miss us in sweet love somehow.
But remember we've gone, not long away.

Days will be easier for you to see.
Good thoughts remain for brother and me.
But we'll be close with our memory.
Then not so far and close we'll be.

We'll miss having our own little room.
We'll miss our rubs like petals in bloom.
We'll miss how warm lying in the hall.
But better for us, now, we have it all.

So don't be sad that we're both gone.
Like you, we'll be together, not alone.
You stay healthy and think about us.
We'll see down to you, not far from us.

Give and Take

Ever watch a flight of Honkers pass over,
The line precision and wing flap speed,
All controlled by the point bird rover?
A clear blue sky will give you the view you need.
Such a perfect "V" as one supports the other!
Who knows where they go as the flight is led.
Who sees that one will not outclimb his brother.
The lift of each is so gracefully read.
Somewhere the uplifted lead will find a place.
His flap will slow and a turn will be made,
As if his direction were on his beaked face,
He will take his group to a little pond or glade.
Circling a few times, the target will be found.
Lower and lower before the split to land,
Each holds until the leader stops the round,
And either a splash or touch will demand.

Winged feathered flight with two feet will retract,
Soaring on the wind with some instinctual pact.
What mystery exists, if learned, how noble the sight.
One need not know a reason if wrong or right.

Oftentimes my car must be steered where others go.
Others depend on my skill to travel the flow—
From this lane to that, there are times of overflow
When so many must find an exit to leave a row.

No one will argue the human brain can learn to reason.
Many choices must be made in a world of give and take—
Whether to abide or make one's life a treason.
A life with no regard how safe we move for others' sake.
Such little effort is made to move or give a try,
In a will to support all other human dignity.
So many times a day when life must not go awry,
Our minds and souls must not lose their moral intensity.

What is there to learn by seeing the graceful birds?
What is found in their beauty to exist together,
The superior human brain can find beyond our words,
By watching them in simple harmony—
These mates of the feather.

Nexus

Looking down on the forest from my searching scenic perch,
The silent morning encapsulates a dawning new scene.
Whether the first light wakened too early puts me in the lurch,
Disenabling the light of day too early shown can mean.
Even the animals so used to hiding from the light
Retain their sheltered place not ready to arise.
That slender moment still undefined makes pause a new right.
Still all must await the covering relating of the skies.
No time to brew the morning cup of coffee, the ritual.
Nothing surpasses the breaking newness of opening day.
Many life-shining renewals can be known between life virtual,
And the actual necessary risings of life's way.
Soon the virgin young fir tops will wiggle to purport lift.
A bear will appear to stretch herself brushing by a tree.
Her brown body will awaken little cubs ready to drift.
Above a hawk will fly, anticipating preys to see.
That moment star of light and warmth will find its full refrain.
The flora and fauna external break will start life's gain.

Persisting Kingdoms

From the window of a bus parsed shade.
Straying under black-fingered branches,
Flick by the little square-windowed view.
The sun's everlasting scorch made
Space between the trees only few chances
To repair to a satiating breeze.

Rare unadulterated density,
Persisting kingdoms free within the bush—
Passing trees topped for elephant food
Suggests domains of stark propensity
To exist in a land where heaven's push
Does not determine life's breach to intrude.

Now and then a single primate stands by
The road, callously haunched, observes
Strange vehicles, bright curiosities
Sweeping through on the asphalt, dry
Under cloudless canopied transport curves,
He watches human monstrosities.

Ahead trees diminish to a park lot.
Tired riders step out on the hard ground.
Off to the side is a dilapidated zoo.
Unmolested hidden close from this spot
Are many living creatures all around,
Unencumbered by what these humans do.

Much less than a Barnum & Bailey draw,
An enterprising penurious hand
For an African fee welcomes us all.
Through a wobbly gate in expected awe
Guiltless hopefuls stride in our little band
To view enclosures spread about large and small.

A tawny coat draws me to a tall fence.
Resting in the morning haze a feline,
Large as a horse sprawls on the concrete block
Indifferent, suggesting no offense.
A male nearby continues his recline.
Queen and king give me pause to take stock.

Not noticing a thick bush, fence entwined,
Concentrating attention on the two,
Another huge cat lies in its shade.
From exhaling sleep, breathes on my mind.
So close is his space, I will not walk through.
How close we are lets me know I strayed.

Noah made the room for all, two by two.
Beasts and the birds came forth and persisted.
The sun and the moon for all life came through.
Great wonder in this world we've all existed.

Without Destination

Flapping wings, skimming, surfing over the waves—
If he could speak, what observations would he make?
Yet he was going so fast no pictures were saved.
Such a straight line he flew that no image would take.
The cool evening just before dusk made no sense.
He had had all day to fling himself straightforward—
Almost all the way across he went, so intense.
He had not been startled, nothing in that regard.
Was he streaking fast ahead for a calmer spot,
One he could float or fish his instinctual fit?
Did he remember time or place, his own known plot
That caused him to fly to an old floating sit?
He did flutter a pull-up and touch down again.
His previous rest was noticed from his take-off,
Which was so quickly graceful where he had been
That appeared so effortless as he darted aloft.
From my human eyes his grace was so attractive,
I tried to put myself in his tumultuous escape,
If that is what it was made me so protractive—
I mean, the way he covered the space like a tape,
Measuring to such a direct lengthened location.
I can remember when I was a kid running fast.
At least, at the time, my mind had little speculation—
I just ran across a field long as I could last.
No reason, I guess, just ran without destination.

The Swallow

Was this little bird surveying us?
Or were we in our cart in his way?
The grass fairway, finely cut and clear,
Wide and rimmed on one side with trees plus,
We obtrusively shared, that golf day.
His open flight had been free, not near.

Fluttering and soaring up and around,
Against a sunny morning, cloud free,
Brightness suggested extending oneself.
Look out over the fresh-fashioned round
Even when the design was ours to see.
Wildlife did not need some noble shelf.

In front of us, above us, beside,
Both were distracted where to go—
His coverage then uncertain, blocked.
We wishing not to break his power glide—
Like he was flying to remove a foe,
And we lunging when our brakes were locked.

His and our impatience grew,
Closer he came to our small windshield
And seemed more often we dodged.
Stop and go, deviate, where he flew
We found his route all over the field.
Our golf bags became camouflaged.

His movements came less aerobatic
As we determined our predestined green.
We supposed he allowed us our way.
Our travels then became less erratic.
Had we ungraciously marred his scene,
And did we intrude on him that day?

Homeward we discussed his winged plight,
Or our selfish weal of his domain—
Each course disrupting the other
In what some might term our little fight.
How anxious we vouchsafed our terrain—
Our condescending caution going further.

Heavy traffic plagued us traveling home.
Impatience grew when some drove too slow.
Power thrives on our roads to our wants.
How courageous we grant freedom's roam.
How oft minds seem to disturb the flow,
Even when we perceive but little taunts.

Indecision

Out of place seemed the little two-lane road,
After freeway driving and side ditches.
Easing to see small farms in slower mode
And the calm, cultivated land riches.

Back from the highway brightly painted houses,
Porches fronted by tree-lined care mown lots—
Rural sentient scenes their sight arouses,
And pride of farm life shown in gorgeous plots.

Glimpses gave way to distant scans.
Grazing cattle, storage barns, and feeding troughs,
Separated acreage, farm demands,
Hills, grain fields outstretched the hay barn lofts.

Glad the road ran straight for these scenic styles—
Their copious spaces enamored our souls.
Absorbed so were we in these natural miles
That we wished we could change our city roles.

Up ahead made no sense since so endowed
Were we held in captive expanding trance.
Like a trail I steered, our car direction bowed
To the narrow black-top reluctant advance.

Then it seemed our hypnotic journey stalled
When ahead, there, something off to the side
Moved and broke out being so enthralled.
So unexpected, I made slower our ride.
From behind a tree came this reaching nose.
We slowed to a stop to further see a doe.
Almost out on the road this beauty froze.
Staring, each found no willingness to go.
Then, with a wistful step, another by its flank
Appeared, stopped, and discovered we were there.
We sat quite still, both of equal rank,

In noble poise, then crossed in tandem pair.
(What had helped them ignore our sudden luck?
But courage of thought could need an anchor.)
To our surprise next stepping out was a buck,
Large and proud carrier of multiple antlers.
He strode gracefully, charming our day.

Allowed to have seen this regal display,
When somehow was the sense we helped that day,
We looked long after they had gone away,
And were pleased they perhaps had gone astray.
The open fields pleasant to them also,
Subject to strangely divided motor flow,
Gave them pause in their ranging places to go.

Such natural presence to feel freedom
Gave us a reminder this life remains
Within our carefully cultured kingdom—
That gifts still are found in casual refrains.

III

MORE THAN NOW

In general, whether a given idea shall be a live idea depends more on the person into whose mind it is injected than on the idea itself.

—William James, 1906

Climb the Apple Tree

One day I decided to climb this apple tree.
Not knowing why I was impelled to do it,
Found myself supposedly needing this vantage to see—
Whatever was that doused me with this slight fit
Of adventure to see farther than I could before.
Sometimes, I guessed, one needs to just explore
That which doesn't appear to be obvious in front
Of all that is there without any ulterior to confront.
But this day there I was bumping into an occasional apple,
Finding a hand or foothold on a limb to grapple.
Unable to satisfy, I kept trying to climb higher
Than this quite large tree, being a supplier,
Could provide me with a place to stop and look.
I supposed I could see farther through a book,
Though one finds physical stress sometimes more exciting.
I could not doubt that this corpulent frame was so inviting.
Anyway, I proceeded to climb up this great old tree,
Finally arriving at a suitable place to stand,
Where I felt like a kid again so attainably free
To precariously stop and view the spread-out land
That lay before me on the edge of that old golf course.

I reflect now as I think passively on that youthful urge
That once was this spirited unexplainable force
To mount, at my age, with some attempt to, at a point, purge
From my soul that physical age
Was only a necessary step on life's unraveling stage.
Two important things from that experience came to appear:
While life exists all motion is a stretch,
Whether a physical or visual search, do not fear—
Something, happily, regardless impels one to catch
The distance to make all out there come clear.

Cypress Knees

The sun was breaking over the tops of the fields,
As we went in leaving the highway behind.
The morning light was raking for new corn yields,
Making some green bows grow for our road to find
The soft surface dirt of the old lake road cut,
Causing our slip and slide through this parted rut.

Close on our bumper trailed his homemade boat
He had built same as others through the years.
Seeing it brought wonder if it would still float,
But he knew after joyous times were no fears.
Dip net to dip net big mouth bass had slipped.
Like paddled water had languorously dripped.

Circling around in the early morning lull,
Setting the brake so not to rub the old lake,
The tackle was placed in the shallow hull
With fresh water we did not forget to take.
We walked back, releasing the little boat hitch,
Pushed off the trailer down a narrow ditch.

Into the small two-man skiff we stepped wide,
Securing a seat on either end, me first,
For I was not old and knew little how to ride.
But he with gunneled flat blade waved a burst
Of paved water behind the boat to the other side.
Through then-rustled water he shoved across
To the other side "to give the plugs a toss."

Eagerly bracing, there were the cypress trees
Standing gaunt, out of water in clustered groups.
They were up straight, not like other chilled trees,
Leafless yet with whitish feet. "Lake washed troops"
I thought as I quick tied my top water bait,
Ready to toss by a bald cypress and wait.

What freedom to make a cast, such peace to pause
And with the beauty of an old simple art
Rejoice in being with such skill, absent cause,
To join his talented pleasure and take part.
Pleasing him, whom I dearly loved, that day
Be with him and strive to his great gifted play.

From time to time, he directed me, "Chunk here!"
Dutifully, I would place it as best I could
Past the knee and draw with care just there,
Hoping to snag the big bass he said I would.
When I had missed, he would strike for a bite.
Even the wily fish could not escape his rite.

Today, only a memory remains to learn
An answer to why he had shared with me.
It was not his art I had striven to earn;
It was not about fishing to observe and see.
Now I know as age has given, I suppose,
This was his only way he knew to be close.

The Nail

Still there was that hole in the post,
Not split when it was driven in,
Though it had been for a long pause.
How much rain, snow, or wind had most
Made weak the wood could not say when
From being hammered for what cause.

Just how came to notice the hole
That day when I stood close to it,
A place to lean in morning thaw.
No inkling except, save my soul,
Stopped to look with nowhere to sit
To look off a hill down a draw.

Sunlight shown calm above the town.
A shadow worked across the post
Adorning its gothic height posed tall,
Lone standing with a hammered crown.
Missing was a cross piece long lost
Years likely dropped a tumbling fall.

One time post holes must have been made
To plant some poles and peen them down
To be seen below by all who would.
But they were gone save this one laid.
Blackened by storms now a coal brown
Seemed blotched and hued like dried blood.

Leaning support in my morning gaze
I raised my hand to prop my arm.
A finger found a small square hole.
Backing into the obscuring haze
A quick flash summoned my alarm:
What had I touched that searched my soul?

A Red Wall

Multi-storied buildings enclosing streets,
Connecting bridges over a river canal,
War memorials adorned with bronze sculptures—
Many in dispute from past political feats;
Noticed by tourists, seen as banal,
Past repulsive domos now dormant ruptures.

A bustling, busy, struggling city,
Diversion moving in separate ways.
Tourists coming to see what was,
And those who know, disguising pity.
Commerce seeming to flourish days,
And nights for the young, a wander buzz,
Boys in other world's sports clothes fits
And teenaged girls in uplifting brassieres
Above peeking navels and skin-tight pants.
Freedom jammed after flagged fears
As the nights become a circuited dance.
Highlighted and noticed by all who come
With visions of the tall red wall,
A bastioned brick fortress called Kremlin,
Standing as a stately and protective conundrum—
Resistance to a world lead pitfall.
This lengthy sculptured massive gremlin,
Concealing like some dynastic sprite,
Isolating but a prominent show.
A past, a false presence continuing,
A giant stepback to hold forthright,
To portend for the world to know
There still exists this dominant entrenching.

So much teased me to how I felt—
Wonder how soldiers booted the cobblestones,
Marched over them with slapping goosesteps.
Band played, red colors flew so svelte—
So many exaggerated tones,
Lights and shades of armament reps.
Then one day, now, the show is past.
Now just the hollow that was stands.
Teenagers and tourists flock by—
So many pass what could not last.
Now a rush to quiet old demands.
Now red and bronze beneath the sky,
Reflecting a time caught and passed.

The ending corner, St. Basil's lack—
A sensed glance before the underpass,
My mind remained without remorse—
The memory skulked at my back,
And a partial eclipse, a trespass
To leave and forget this false force.
And then below once more to light
There came a little tug at my cuff.
A little gypsy child wiggled my pants,
Just ruble to make things right.
A saddened flinch made me rebuff,
A mother waited that angered my chance—
An old light plugged my provoked stance.
A tear now seems to have rent my soul.
This injury now I must live to control.

The Battle Won

As a boy I walked through the weeds;
Like wheat grain dry in summer heat,
They whisked my pant legs as if pleads
Sounded when under my booted feet
I mashed them flat making a trail,
After crushing a tunnel through.
Little thought about how dry and frail
My tromping feet left for anyone who
Might come looking for me later.
As I trod the waist-high tan spikes,
Not thinking of any need to be safer,
I was the soldier on his hikes
Into this vast untamed country.
I was the captain of my own domain,
Surveying my landlocked boundary,
Exploring my claim, it would remain
My kingdom, my time to give search
As the world's great leader to find
Undiscovered places of great worth
For my presence to free mankind.
This still time gave no breezy sweep
To wave the weeds or bend the tops.
No sound stirred by warm latent air
Stretching and swirling nature's crops.
Only stilting dry brush despair
Gave no resistance on my way,
As I waved my hands parting space
To seek my adventure that day.
Sometimes my extended fingers touched
Straw ends stiffly scraping my open hand,
But they were subordinates pushed
In groups having to bend their stand.
All-powerful, all-knowing I marched
Through forces unable to stop me.
I stroked away all the sun-scorched
Troops who were no match for my free

Will to move its determined length.
Tireless in my sole battle fought,
Youthful spirit drove my strength
Toward whatever goal I sought.
Mine was the life of a warrior,
None to fear from inferior foes;
A world vanquished by a superior,
A juggernaut wielding fatal blows.
The measured horizon gave no chance,
By the evenly reflected sun's
Clear inevitable advance,
Of defeat by an enemy's runs.
Then in the battle won, a pause
To survey the field came half done
A moment to dream of my cause.
A voice at my back broke my fun:
"Come, son, it's time to go home."

Ocean Shores

Beyond the simple little painted light post—
(It stands over the remnants of a scraggly lawn)
Beneath my window, sitting and munching my toast,
A small light marks a look to scan the dawn.
Through the spreading opening of a mini-cloud sky,
Just out farther than beach grass cluttered patches of broom—
Out there somewhere must be a trail to pass by
The salal and other tall faded free bushes making no room—
There can be seen about a quarter of a mile away
A man (or woman) struggling or pushing to trudge through
The wild growths that govern the hiker's anxiety delay,
To reach a long lateral mound proving an obstructive view.
An arching back and uplifted face is drawn to the light;
But, if not careful, another bush is so tall it blurs,
And the seeker must go around to keep in sight
That uneven horizontal pushed-up preventer to climb over.
Of course, my grand omnipotent perspective is all-seeing.
From my comfortable perch, there is no ungainly distraction,
Save a crow with difficulty ducking, flies by fleeing
The quickness of a swift smaller bird mad at some infraction.
(The smaller pursues the slower soarer, causing his
      dissatisfaction.)

How high must any of us have to elevate ourselves to go
Through all things and those that keep us from moving
Our own chosen paths to, as has been said, the flow
That each of us adopts to help our determined improving?

From my position one can see over the mound,
The rolling white foaming breakers flowing toward the bumpy
      ground.

One can see the vast silver-gray sea stretched in the distance.
As daylight is mysteriously awakened to the upper reaches,
There are now more searchers, more intrigued. For instance,
One preference is to view before finding its worth.
Wonder what it is that draws one to see it
Up close?—Maybe it's to be a part or find some new birth.

Each has to examine whether to walk out or to sit.
Looking from an overviewing allows many considerations,
But so does going out and getting close to the motion.
(Whether to read or grasp this supply of reiterations
Is a choice to decide where one can be to view the ocean,
When and where people go to observe it, and if they do,
Time and place to discover what penetrates the mind.)
All things are there and many can be seen through
By a walk in the bush or over the hill, if one is so inclined.

Nothing can prevent a sublime run of the senses,
Or the determination to find either with body or heart,
Can walk out or up to and around all fences;
But not to act or refuse to make a start,
May cause one to miss the potent joys of inspection
That can come from a time and space reflection.

Pecan Memories

There were those days seemingly not too long ago, when—
When we all, on a somehow no-wind wintry day
Piled in the old car and drove out of town to begin
Riding over an open gravel road, not too far away,
To go out into the country—my mom, dad, and I,
To go to a place my dad knew about near the river:
Where we could turn off the road below an open clear sky,
And find those old trees we could see from the fliver—
That were loaded with dry bent hickory limbs.
Those branches would be so full of oval, smooth shelling covers
That just seeing them you could almost taste beneath the
    sheaths,
Over the oily sweet edible kernels, you could discover.
We were there to pick them off the ground.
There were those that loosed and had fallen from above,
And those we stick-knocked down and easily found.
It was for me a celebration of something fun to do.
It was a time to be together—my mom, dad, and I were
    together.
Looking back now it was a happy moment we went through—
A happy moment when three sensitives were birds of a feather.
Wonderful memory given to me to fortify and last.
Love was then and now a memory, which reconstitutes the
    past—
Beautiful memories give continuity to the soul.
They are more than a thoughtful journey of the spirit.
This one took me back to a time when I didn't just play a role,
But was joined with others who did not fear it—
Who enjoyed each other as we stretched and smelled the river
    air
Against the musty trees, which had grown old.
It was a time that gave me a loving memory to spare,
One that I can call on to bring me back into the fold,
And give me needed feelings that have become rare.

Nature's Harbingers

There's something about trees at night,
Or bushes reflecting in the evening light.
(They make the evening a time to excite.)

Something is encouraging for them to be there.
A shiny leaf can do more and signal where
Life exists with ample beauty to spare.

So accustomed we, from day to day, become
Immune to the greenery that sparkles for some,
And just there for any Jane and Tom,

Who may be too busy to stop and admire
How any ol' plant, even a prickly sweetbrier,
Can add to the evening landscape and bring fire

To the eyes and heart when viewed with life's desire
To grasp the natural contrasted with things that expire.
Oh, to find the shrub that marks the place to retire.

Beside a tree, or next to a deep green plant,
You can feel the tender life and somehow can't
Make sense of it all if you rave and rant.

There's too much wasted time feeling things
When the secrets are hidden in ardent flings,
When nature's harbingers stretch wiser strings.

Buffeting Currents

Many miniature mountains of gray water whitecapped,
Sighted through a drizzled blurry glass,
Prowing toward a safer route carefully mapped—
A power ride slotting through areas whales pass.

The fast craft, a sleek modern passage conveyance,
Slashes deliberately through a bedeviled riptide.
The straits give back a rocking convergence.
It searches and plows, rending problems subside.

Life has such buffeting currents at times,
Covering with windy and cold gray skies;
But human ingenuity conquers many disturbed climes,
Only to make smoother countless travailing tries.
Onward we must go wherever a weathered path defies,
Till a destination is seemingly more easily reached,
And other challenging entries are breached.

More Than Now

Everything changes—
They say, but is it true?
Heard someone important say so.
Who knows but see it through.
Look, they say, existent things grow—
May be, stick around and see.
Some don't believe; some disagree.

Everything arranges—
From every rut to every road,
Look and feel each bounce change.
Life grows and each weighty load
Creates for us depressant images strange;
But the image can only appear—
Soon it is gone; images disappear.

Everything exists—
More than now; more than sight.
Strain to see; develop it right.
They say each thing reaches over—
Notice that life completes the exposure.
So why stir about and worry—
What now must be; what's the hurry!

Everything persists—
The tree persists through the season.
Relax the shape; let it grow.
Poets can muse about the reason.
Search the soul and one can know
There's a time to come and go.
Let us just be and live to know.

Something More

Start with a walk in the morning.
Begin with a stroll in the borning—
A first glance at the shining through
The dark air's offering disappearing anew.

That morning came with a grouch and a creak.
It was my mind resisting a move and a peek
From the stored-up anxiety the day before.
It hung so that urged me resist all in store.

A day must begin with new hope, not despair.
A way will open even though rumblings try to impair
Another chance to present itself. Take a heart,
The problems will subside, so make a start.

The other day was the other day.
Today is not, look and smell a fresh display.
See all that God is putting on your tray—
Let a new perception receive the vast array.

When I started out, she helped me
Weave in and let my mind open out to see
The many possibilities around to believe.
She helped me wonder what to conceive.

We two strode the journey taken before,
But now was different and new to explore.
(She helps me each time beyond the door—
When will I help her find something more?)

Your Own Felt Need

Often is heard the need to be there
On time, if you will, for some reason or other.
Ever thought what a grip that will ensnare?
A catch is then made; don't extend any further.

The moment is taken; refusal is not given.
One suddenly feels a sense of being driven.
No case will be accepted if one does not comply.
Expectations are put out so you try—
So you squeeze and fight through congestion
And unseen happenings never allowed in question.

To make it never a great feat,
All consider that "making it" is a repeat
Of all those other times when you didn't fail,
You were always ever faithful, like the mail,
As long as taken as duty there would be no doubt,
When all occurred, regardless of what it was about.

Then one day when you thought you could,
And you felt the pressure and promised you would,
Things stacked up against your very determined will
And you pushed yourself forward trying still
To do what you had seemed to have done before—
Just do what you would, not what others deplore.

Determine to discover your own felt need.
Consider to strive where you can succeed.
To allow others to create tests for you
Is not the world that permits you inside.
Do what you wish, explore your own stride,
For it has been given you only to decide.

The Tulip Hues

The color was what enticed us
To make the once-a-year drive by,
The clear contrast was worth the fuss
And anticipation of color grown to mystify.

The uniformity of them made us gaze
Every time we journeyed to reach the fields,
Away from the artificial city haze
And find such brilliant cultivated yields.

Colors are often blended and subdued
In the everyday landscapes of our lives;
But once seen, specified light leaves us glued
To the deep contrast absences our hope derives.

Just once lets us know of this picturesque absolute,
Even though humans have had to grow it.
Among all the mish-mash we become resolute,
And solve complexity as we know it.

Passerby

I saw a singular cloud pass another one by,
As if none were important in the sky.
It took a time of course to make the pass
With not so much a trace or show of class
Did the passerby let on the other was there,
Not even a deviation or a wind current stare.
Often wonder, when passings fail a salute,
What others may feel who witness such a route?
Do others think only one world is this;
Or do they see that in particular is amiss?
Maybe it's just one observer's sensitivity
To find one with such exclusivity,
To pick one which does not notice another.
It's sure one could attest to be directed hither.
I mean one attends to a place, not act whither
Any place is supposed more important than another;
But if this is taken important by a brother,
A tilt or a swift would be taken right there.
Just to dip hello or glad to see you where
We all find ourselves in this grand scheme together,
Not like we were each some wind-blown feather.

Blurred Locus

The target appeared a splash of red.
The hit was cleared; no more was said.
The drive became no more an aim
To reach the green now less a claim.
To size the putt was hard to focus
On the hole in front. A blurred locus
Seemed to draw the ball away to charm
My mind and make me lose my arm
That must be straight to follow through
And tap the ball on a line that's true.

Planter's Gain

Two broadleafed trees planted side by side—
An arranged opportunity for both to reside.
Subject to be planted their pre-grouped way
Gives each the strength for the other to stay.
Whatever is given off from the sweeping wind
And the rain and flying things for them to fend,
They resist those forces that would push them out
From the places chosen that fill us with doubt.
Praise that they stand each year they remain.
We admire their strength for the planter's gain.

Fixation

I stood there looking, observing unsullied nature
With ancient mountain peaks out front of my window.
Down from the virgin trees across an expanse of stature,
Through road crossings interrupting green flow,
My mind was stilled, unable to take it all in—
Eyes transmitted mixed messages to my heart,
While fixed pointedly on aged reminders, when
The wearing forces were unable from the start
To wear down but somehow wear up
The highest visuals of snow-spattered elevations.
Motionlessly standing alone taking a full sup
Of all I could compare from life situations,
My free thinking staggered an endless moment—
Not remembering when first I stood to look.
My body began to quiver and thought to foment
How the physical feeling as read from a book,
The beginning that led through a plot of reason,
Leading to reflection of why it all began.
It seemed my heart stopped from some treason
Of time and fixation between nature and man.

Something from Somewhere

There the bleached senescent earth is under your feet.
Stretched further form outcropped dried bush trees,
The dirt lies uneven with innumerable unsettled depressions.
You stand while residents there often sit with nothing to
    repeat—
No stories unless stories move the spirit that frees
The mind for some loosened remembered confessions.

Temperatures are not noticed for the night,
Which approaches and arrives with little distinction.
The whitish soil defines carelessly the felt heat
As it gives way a little to the slow daily flight
The sun makes imperceptibly rendering the woods brittle—
Rubbing against a limb cracks like a cracker element of
    intinction.

When the sun finally slips away from a distant view,
You will develop an ancient awareness of a glorious presence.
Looking out the shadowed land appears strangely hollow—
The darkness sheds no fear, only a drawing to the true
Vision unspoiled by what man uses artificially below.
What was bleak now compels a startling essence.

Up to see, your eyes reach a beauty so wonderfully vast.
This gift is given only to those who struggle to live.
Here is this place where sun and stars design
Exist for as long as those souls who live there must last.
Something from somewhere suggests this is there to give.
None are forgotten and all reign sublime.

The Gift of Night

Sitting quietly with the senses of the evening peace,
The quelling shadow seems to mark that noises cease
And outside fragrances are compliments to loving embrace;
From the blasts of day's chaos of a tangled race
To expel the highs and lows of all measuring woes,
We speak of opposites as contrasting day with night.
But the same continuous life exists in shadowed light
Through all the hours that span both light and dark.
What can be seen somehow portrays day's ignited spark.
Too bad for a word misspoke to seek the calm of evening,
An expected time ensconced we have need of agent leavening—
Nature's turning of the earth for most a change
To reflect on the thoughts of contacts to rearrange
For a more favorable verbal touch to those we met,
And reconfigure their misconcept we came to regret.
The gift of the night comes to us as a blessing
And a space in between to prepare our own confessing,
Projected to the morrow to relieve the sorrow,
Occurrences for new thoughts on reflections we can borrow.
Whether those we were with may have misconceived,
Sensitivity for good feelings we have time to conceive.

An Ode

A place to sit, a place to read,
Two terms compatible, both concede.
Which comes first, a small decision,
But both in comfort, a likely condition.
Two to become, two from recourse.
A right to grow, negotiate a source.
A passive action, a sensitive reaction.
The need to know for great satisfaction.
A pleasure found, a transferred thought,
Some measured expression could be wrought.
Vicarious experience, life lived from another.
One step forward to venture further.
A human creation, a skill to be earned,
At an age can be learned.
A melding of physical with the mental
Presents worlds of life transcendental.
Whether analytic or just a journey,
Destinations are found, searches for eternity.

A Path to Learn

To be clear is an art of devotion richly brought
To all who wish to write the cogent text.
With will to seek from word struggles fought,
A quality of expression from words and rules fixed,
Which may, in the search, surmount all forms tried,
Since passing mass meaning is often denied.

Yet the way to express the complexity sent,
And the will to find the skill to scribe
A message of truth with little deviant bent,
From a seeker after some private diatribe,
Is mental work not often easily grasped
From those before with talent unsurpassed.

But to learn from others who have succeeded,
To study the use their words have been put,
And the toil allowed for them to go unimpeded,
Must be known by those who would place a foot
On lengthy path, given the time and diligence,
An image of passion could step with intelligence.

A final reward can come when the task to travel
Has been taken to gain all one can find
In the trek through books and journals to unravel.
One day the triumph may come from the kind
Of work that may be read and believed,
From practice and talent—an education received.

Why Wish to Go

Climb to heights up a farther reach,
But when to stop is hard to know.
From young to old the work to teach
Comes to most how far one can go.
Why just to climb for goal and till
To move here to there up the hill?

Saw a neighbor contract some work—
"Rebuild my steps," said he to him,
"Build them higher." A strange quirk.
It seemed to me he reached the rim,
Already as high to touch the landing.
Meant he wants for higher standing?

Treading up some steps will be a higher gain,
If that is where he wished to go,
If he cannot rest or remain
In place to live the to and fro.
When steps are not so spelled out,
Much less is told what life's about.

But we go on, step to the end.
What place that is to work and strive.
Some good must come from trying to send
All others to go and try arrive.
Until some thought is given to know,
Marching upward means most to grow.

Life Is Not a Game

It's only a game, so they say.
What makes a game are the rules.
Often thought a game is only display—
People playing, organizing their tools
To outwit, control, and try to win,
Only to end and try, try again.

But others will say, and they try
To use some rules and tend to play,
And make it seem one must comply,
If goals are made to lead a way.
Each step becomes a certain bridge
To reach a point, complete a pledge.

What is game, so often played
That drives a player in so deep,
And draws such energy more often staid,
Until a goal from strength must reap.
Effort and will must not outlast
Those values held from an honest past.

Life's not a game, we should know,
Not something played to make steps.
Each person acts for all to grow.
Not man-made rules or concepts
Can govern spirit and soul to live.
No game exists for life lived.

Let It Out

Keep it in, let it out.
What to do, life is about—
A dilemma of all mankind
Consciously brought for all to find.

Beautiful flower all closed in on itself,
Waiting for assistance from the world without—
Awaiting the sun's rays to touch its outer shelf,
As we all wait for its time not to pout—
Not to hide its open face for all of us to see.
Its full extension is all it will ever be.

Human nature exists to use its potential,
To reach out and search for all it may give,
To find scope and delivery so influential.
From each spirit comes a surge to live
And must not be held from all to use.
Essences are lost when we refuse.

Dream Hole

To open one's eyes to the deep silent night
After all actual care and wear has pervaded,
Where the edge of conscious decisions is one's plight,
And the mystery of begin and end has invaded—
There is no song to sing but to muse the brink.
From what seemed to be but then must remember,
What train of life has passed through, we think,
Of what noisy melody has made such an illogic dismember?
Consciousness cannot grasp the fading dream-hole escape
From the conclusions of the day that tracked the mind.
But regardless of the strange episodic break,
There was a release of a meandering kind
That exposed this reverie and opened back
To marvel at this unconnected mental state,
And felt the pleasure to become aware and track
The two and know that both are there to contemplate;
That were it not for some divine manufacture,
What would life be with such a drastic fracture?

An Unfriendly Sport

Time tires of misery that mocks
The mistakes recorded by clocks
Of each day that withholds the hurt
And stymies forgetfulness words insert
Into the panoply of public mirth
After misspoken meaning of no worth—
Embarrassment's byproduct of mental haste
From irritated interruption of ego waste.
More than the wrong verbal release
Is the felt sense of a fractured peace
That the mind will not loose
From long after its malaffective use.
Sensitivity to this verbal mistake
And reactive care for a human sake
Will ease the rueful self-inflicted retort
And the time not be an unfriendly sport.

Look Behind

The weekend came and off they went,
With the car loaded and family content,
To go to the mountains, a happy place
They'd been before, a day to retrace—
The sights and smells of a glorious space.

A special Saturday, they would take all day,
Rising early, the wagon hummed a time to play.
To the outskirts, trees marked the way.
Douglas firs grew numerous to guide them
And then peaks cleared, arose to greet them.

The hills came higher and curves swung wider.
They did not hurry, excitement their provider.
For their favorite place, they thrilled to return.
Going there was special; they retraced, relearned
The things they recalled in alder and fern.

There was a stream where they would stop.
Suddenly, there, up ahead, over the top
Of a bridge rising and falling, turn here,
There was their spot to set the gear.
A moment they paused, bank was still sheer.

Out of the car, dropped the back door.
The clothes and food spread across the floor—
Special things for all to unload and share.
They amused themselves and ventured to dare
To find a trail and inhale the forest air.

The day slipped away, shadows started to grow.
Back to the car, over the bridge to go,
But something happened to make Dad think;
A surprise occurred, a thoughtful link
That made him pause, a life he shrank.

Began playing games, he became the leader,
He happened upon a railroad feeder
Track since forgotten, stretching through the growth.
There beside a trail, parts hidden from both.
Childhood returned, balancing he went,
Down the rusted span, almost heaven sent.
Finding his own joy, quite carelessly bent,
And then he heard, knowing not how long
He'd walked the track, there came a song.
Breaking the trance, he looked behind,
And there she was, closing slowly behind.

Sometimes it takes forgetfulness to see
When selfishness will become not meant to be.
The chosen life escapes a love to have,
Can be resurrected and become a salve,
Love soothing cherished life, the care we have.

After the While

He stood staring off shore, out to sea.
As I saw him, I thought why stare
Out from that stand in such degree—
No moment to dodge the sun's glare,
He seemed locked on some point out there.

To be still serves the mind in search
For time to think and while the day.
Eyes find no touch, nothing to besmirch—
Nothing distracts the well, which may
Be in tune with some other display.

He did not move his body or head.
He was transfixed; he saw no sight—
Some inner mirage where other seems fed
From sources intact, his own delight.
His face was calm, the moment was right.

The sea rolled in, small waves topped out,
Little crested ripples slid to their end.
Now and then birds darted round about,
Then and again a raindrop would descend.
No rise and fall seemed to offend.

He stood so long made me wonder:
What internal fire, what strange desire?
Was it the sea, its sound to ponder,
That took his mind an instant to inspire;
That little strand of time to transpire?

And then he moved, seemed he would not.
Suddenly, he looked from side to side
As if to come awake from that spot
Where life and dream would not collide.
After the while, he now could abide
Whatever he could and went to decide.

Two Trimmers

To take it down,
part of the fence
was dismantled carefully.
Two trimmers worked,
one spiked up to the top,
the other stayed by
and stood waiting
for parts to fall.
First the top tipped
over into the lot.
The sky was left
open to see.
Then another plummeted.
Soon it was cleaned
to be sawed
into suitable blocks,
and stacked.
Limbs into the shredder
were stoked and disposed.
The fence parts
were nailed back
in place as before.

The earth was left
to clean
what was now debris,
lopped and hacked.
Now no blowing winds
could tear the fence
from their force—
delicate things are
protected to control
the flow man made.
What clutter becomes
either verbal first
and then contractual.

But what is a tree?
Above, all its beauty,
it must come down.
Each year,
some filled with leaves,
others bare limbed
to mark the seasons
and measure
all the gentle turns.
We are reminded
of all the heights
of grace and flow.

Who decides,
and from what decisions
must come.
Structure crashes from structure.
Human construction
and nature's growth—
purpose over beauty!
Who will finally know
what is there,
and what could be?

Dawned Trespasses

Protected from the days' world and dawned trespasses,
Unseen measures of interaction create an unleashing sense,
Driven to malicious acts from mysterious crevasses,
Inflicting invidious stealth from sources crying recompense.
For decisions of false freedoms taken may evince
An aftermath spawned blight of some resulting morass.

The darkness of meaningful thoughts with motives concealed,
And invoking verbal and nonverbal actions of distrust,
Shows missing character from that which is unrevealed.
For respect is shown when actions are internally just—
Fruit from shiny covers, as beauteous fruit unpeeled,
May not be found sweet under a colorful crust.

Pleasure can come after the nights of repose,
When days are found and clarity has been presented,
And truth is visible when daylight can disclose
Before what was said resulted from the consented.
Strength of self is fortified when trust represented
Gives knowledge of love from the friends of those.
Not knowing from the apple what would occur,
One morning at breakfast another had similar wants.
Wondering if an apple and my taste would concur,
Outside, early, the birds flew from the squeaky taunts
Of a little creature with soft gray fur.
Like me, he mused for breakfast an apple yet green
Might from his limb be just the thing.
After his balanced chews, he did something strange.
He dropped down, splayed in the dry leaves,
Unable to walk or shinny other trees.

Sometimes the fruit appears to be so appealing,
Not knowing the taste from the covering seen—
Engulfs our judgment and interrupts our feeling,
We cannot know what another might truly mean.

Unforsaken

Sighting comes in variform beats on a busy crowded street,
Walking or standing becomes a chosen observable feat
To hold in temporary glances; the reflecting mind explodes
With singular visions of circumstances where want erodes
Into directions and misdirections for deviations one must take
In a swirl of winding the way into passages one must make.

A bystander has first to look for a best place to stand and see
The throngs of surveyors in a busy world appearing to be free.
Many single minds dart here and there to escape the hindering
Travels to this shop and that amidst many others' meandering.
But a place to stop, look, and think of moves erratically
  seeming,
To see the attracting commerce, one can find some scheming.

A gained perspective of journeys in which many others strive
Requires a view of one then another in struggles to arrive
At a place someone wants to go to prospect one more station
That evokes a will to make it once through with
  determination—
A view of so many trudging such cumbersome routes taken
Reveals a too tensive world in a time we have not forsaken.

Bounds of Beauty

Where can beauty be found within the earth's contour?
All within the bounds of contact wherever it may be—
The eyes, the ears, the touch, the heart, and more,
Can be resolved in conscious witness to infinity.
Does one seek it because it was found before?
Was it one time there and now looked for again?
And why is told in some forgotten lore
As something there was known only sometime when?
Is not a plant or tree always beautiful?
And even in its various stages it marks the seasons
For all to find regardless of insentient dutiful
Scarping of surfaces yielding to human reasons.
Is not the quality of life paralleled in a tree?
It grows through wind, rain, and nature's perturbations
And in all this, it qualifies when allowed to be free
To stretch its limbs and strength to landscapes' enervations.
Beauty is with us each day and night to see
Into the responses that come from the eternal soul,
And gives us the pleasure sprouting to help us be
A part of the content and context on heaven's role.

Life's Brief Recall

Just look at the leaves as they grow on a tree,
Seem like pinion pieces that want to hang free.
Color is given them, as the seasons pass by
And form contour shapes, help us see a life change.
And when the time comes, detaches and seems to fly
Down on the wings of air floating to rearrange
With a soft settling touch for a velvet lie.
So without weight and substance, bereft of blood,
Take on last a new place-cover like a flood—
A profuse mix of color shed from different trees
Makes a spread of orange, brown, gold, yellow or red.
For a time the yards almost say, "Look now, please.
You will not see me long, for my trees have shed."
A clear special time is about to come again
To bring to all that from the old the new begin—
What we can see from nature's gift to us all
A picture reminder of life's brief recall.

Alone with Engine Sounds

A throat mike snapped to his neck,
Sitting there strapped in his seat,
Looking at the clouds—like puffy specks,
Sailing through the sky. What a feat,
He thought as the engines droned,
And seemed motionless as they flew.
Across the aisle another sat cloned
In his seat, another one of the crew.
As the sun glistened on the wings,
Even the trailing edge sparkled,
Parts of it moving, they were kings—
And then suddenly, he was startled.
A slight blur behind the nacelle—
He had not seen on top before.
What it was, he could not tell,
Since his training had been no more.
Motioning his clone to take a look,
He slid over and searched the spot,
Only to remind the oil it took,
And blur was not a lot.
"Just watch it and note its growth.
If it does, report up front.
Need not worry, we need not both
Be concerned; nothing to confront."

The sun was bright against white clouds.
Over the top of them we soared.
The engine sounds removed all shrouds
Of doubt. Rumors were always deplored,
Must not prevent us from our way.
The gyro compass would not lie;
Their route was sure. We would stay
The course and continue to fly.
The rear bulkhead door was locked.
The air seemed smooth, all was right.

The distance and time were correctly clocked.
Weight was balanced for an even flight.
Adjusting my strap, I would not worry.
In the distance, another plane was alone,
Going the other way, seemed a hurry,
Into a farther cloud, quickly gone.
All by themselves reached into the air.
How clear it was, beautiful to be
Above the earth, much sky to spare.

After sipping some coffee, another glance.
The sun now was not so bright.
Onto the wing from a drowsy trance,
A stain appeared larger in my sight.
An intercom call to the flight engineer
Was a call seemed proper to make.
A young rider called from his fear—
More from reason to not mistake
Than my youth allowed me to know.
Life had been short for my concern.

Oil had been lost, all must return.
Not half the journey had been flown.
A leak was slow. All could learn
From youth, though not yet grown,
Could do better when more was known.

Physical Flaws

He mused waiting,
Internally debating.

The audience was full.
He felt the pull.

People muttered around him.
The chance was slim.

Should he go relieve?
Would they perceive?

The urge would pass.
Show some class.

Mind over body,
Late would seem shoddy.

He must be ready;
His walk must be steady.

He wanted to drink,
But could he think?

How about his posture?
Mouth up some moisture.

Think of good thoughts
Rather than oughts.

Think of applause,
Not of physical flaws.

Think of the text,
Not must be next.

Don't worry how,
Just do it now.

Be on display—
Thoughts win the day.

Make them clear.
Speak without fear.

He must state
Before it's too late.

He's thinking the way,
About to say.

Mind over self,
He told himself.

The Tormenting Splash

An attempt to prevail against a torrent of light splash
Comes when drowsy eyes still have the lingering film of
    sleeping.
The blinds fail to hold the break from sensitive, storied
    weeping.
An extra pillow is beyond reach to stifle the sudden crash.
An arm swings a hand to protract the night from piercing rays
That were imperceptible until they found the narrow slit.
The day came unwelcomed into as contextual memory decays.
Such subconscious essence tries its hold for just a bit;
But the room cannot hold its sanctity for any longer,
Since the hidden corners reappear in the forced light.
Holding back the conscious realm normally comes much
    stronger,
So that the rapture of another plot seems not right.

Which time to think about is explored under pressure
Of another story, an old problem from a forced fissure.

The gnawing ache of a lengthened treasured moment
Like all such times has been found to make an end.
The day such as all days comes again for solutions to foment—
Which of the two was a dream for the dreamer to defend?

Mother's Love

The planter box pansies swirl a romance—
Wistful wriggle from the uphill sea breeze.
We had potted them to withstand by chance
The kinds of weather if dry, cold, or freeze.
Though most days in Spring gusts whistle with rain,
Even bushes are not immune. Bristling leaves,
Like humans, their limbs wiggle, shake off pain,
As if shrubs can feel, so hold who believes.
My mother used to talk to her flowers,
Praising them with verbal caresses.
After wind and rain, garden work took hours.
Her words would condemn wind and rain excesses.
She would make sure the dirt would again be firm—
The too moist ground to be reworked for their feet.
Too much water would lean them out infirm.
She pushed soil with fork or spoon to reseat.
On clear days she would revel among them.
Any season did not deter her giving love
To those whose health when return looked grim.
She would cite the beauty of skies above.
Whether all the mingling flowers she knew
Stood in dry, cold, or freeze she worked through,
Gave all she could to restore them anew.

A Face of Grace

Straight over the six-lane bridge this morning
The early water looked ice slick, waveless.
All skyscrapers around stood scorning—
Their unwillingness to plunge its smoothness—
As if structures would cause it to swell up
And run like an overflowing coffee cup.
One boat sat out (must have been held, anchored)—
Sitting out from others docked in suspension
Peacefully sitting without city rancor,
As bumper chaffers paid no attention
To a setting off such a hectic pace,
Just over the girded rail, face of grace.

All crossers today must have had flashes—
Visions, images, if this bridge would hold.
Steel bridges like steel skyscrapers might splash,
Might tear apart from some bomb; and once bold,
Would make sad the injury to our country.
Each traveler would see and feel this symbol
While we live in one world, one nation.
To feel such hate and revenge, we tremble:
We wish such evil sent to damnation.
While we go each dawn to earn our day's bread,
We come to expect such allegiance just said.
But higher is freedom's tariff on earth!
Just one globe, one place to occupy a piece.
We take for granted any thought of its worth,
Unless suddenly proud structures would cease—
They could topple into the quiet water
One morning; this morning could be a slaughter.

Such reminders have occurred some place away.
Some place away is not here, not in this place.
This place overlooking, above this placid bay,
Above and staid supporting the human race;
Apart from other people, another culture,
Apart from this view, this space, this structure.
Is crusade fighting still a religious war?
Is such comparison an oxymoron?
Is freedom to choose so strangely so far?
Confused and ignorant others fight on.
Peoples of contrast begin to rattle;
Bubbles expand like spheres of babble
If enough pressure is exerted within.
Bodily missiles spring out as wild darts—
No reason or sense like sparks to begin
Hitting out at order separating parts.
An uncommon imbalance wounds a city;
A vicious impact causes death and pity.

Reflecting the brightening sun of peace—
Silver calm so inviting from the bridge,
A wonderful symbol, a mariner's crease,
In a world of people seeking an edge.
We can come to feel among stark contrasts
That peace can be shared when beauty outlasts.

Local Heroes

To speak *una voce* projects respect
Following a position related,
Discussing a point openly debated.

So much emphasis placed on prominence
Derived from other known experiences
Comes to those who have achieved eminence.

A distinguished military career, praised
Avenues of credited bravery,
Tend to imbue others' attention raised.

Introduced in another locality,
Recognized for worthy accomplishments,
People listen beyond their reality.

To go away for a great length of time
And have fame and fortune caress the soul,
Amorous senses can draw hearts like rhyme.

Stories are told about great successes.
Media renders a plethora of words,
Then images will soar from well-placed verbs.

History transforms the eventual datum.
Learned minds espouse the prolific past
And time therefore relates the die so cast.

Grand events remain sources to dwell upon.
Legends become *sic transit gloria mundi*
But heroes graduate, locales unknown.

A Touch of Love

Rain's gentleness kisses the leafy plants—
Diverted sheen from the sun's stingy trance
Spills the hint of balmy air lean and clean—
Ambiguous strength what weather can mean.
Across the flower tops risen soft haze
Pastes the air to the face like a soft glaze
Temporarily woos an upturned forehead—
Magnetically draws the feel of a soft bed.
The horizon is localized in haste,
As one resents a sun break will soon waste.
A summer time, which reforms delicate heat,
Comes not often but sweet aspired retreat.

The touch of love brings a sense of well-being.
So many ways feelings come not seeing:
Moved in church from words and music blends,
Sensual scenes the mind won't comprehend;
But stay in later day-dreamed distractions,
Warm drinks in cold wind-left contractions
In atmosphere where nostrils breathe in
And memories return not conscious when
The time was lived and something once was felt
That warmed the system and cold fears did melt.

The good earth's setting of life is a gift.
Shrubs, flowers, plants we see seem not to drift—
The soil holds and gives growth as softness spreads
When moisture permeates and holds the threads,
Long enough to be caught and gently swallow
With just the right amount of sun to follow.
Beautiful colors for health and delight
Attach themselves with nature's tender might.
Verdant coverage is seen melded green.
The horizon becomes a distant scene,
Missing the spaces in between *plantae*
Are not observed when viewing distant *scaenae*,

Like a facade life usually is broad strokes,
The faces and lives like plants are not folks,
Just easy to read patches and flocks of spots
Governing the undetailed what-nots.
Though each foliage entity reaches out
Even in the distance they have no clout.
We read through the light haze and summery rain.
Who knows how much each human's sight will gain?

Aggregate Souls

Rolling over the aggregate
with others
in a transport-busy world
going someplace,
in an interlocking stream
all on a clock—
timed distances to reach
someone waiting,
someone already traveled,
landlocked there
interims close following others.
Exasperating!
Wishes come to fly away
into the air,
above the frequency modes
to be then free.

The Season

The season is almost here—
Again a time upon us.
Almost as if we are accustomed
To our decoration fuss.

Downstairs packed away in boxes,
A memory put away,
Filling storage shelves of space
Until time comes to be gay.

Her heart so longs for me
To help usher in the joy.
Be the one—"Let's put things out."
Start the love; keep hearts' employ.

Warm the home with shining lights.
Bring the time back again.
Play the music; sweeten the nights
And harken to that night when.

Why is it called a season?
Why is it almost here?
Love and memory need no reason.
Our souls keep it all year.

Beauteous Worth

Anything whiter than a snow flake,
Frozen crystal fluttering to earth?
Short lived it flies in crowds to make
Holding shape a beauteous worth.

Somewhere the air so cold does freeze.
Water no more will liquid fly.
A drop then changes in blizzard breeze
And slowly floats a spatial try.

In silent trysts each flight follows.
Each sail to land together free,
Pushed as if by heaven's bellows,
Blown around in a swirling spree.

True love doth fly in marital dance
As if they fell in some mystic art,
They come one day to meld in chance
That to unite their end to start.

Chaste they move in most joyful glee,
Descending gladness symphony
Come pure and true for us to see
This blissful group in harmony.

As all about in this I stand,
I feel the freshness of a hand
Touching me with so clean a world,
That lets me see my God unfurled.

Now Time Draws Near

As when once a town crier sounded out his refrains,
Wafting choral music entwined did respond.
Windows and doorways seeped oft sung strains
Heard floating, as on air, found a soothing bond.

Now time draws near with lights hung glowing,
Young and old start to sing more in joy's harmony.
Love's gifts in heart's touch, reached in their flowing,
Lift again in the caring of God's symphony.

Many stars long ago gave off their golden lights,
Shining off the snow seemed a holy azure blue;
Even animals punched holes directly that night
As their drivers' belief pointed the place all knew.

Under the same stars, today's retention exists,
As turmoil tests human souls hold His message,
One signal star to point His, the way still persists;
Yet leads again the same way to find His passage.

Here now when goodwill and peace meet and embrace,
May we seek each other in the kingdom of His love;
And in this gentle time when deep hearts find a place,
May we reach out to each other as that star above.

The Black Knight

The night's splendor has no feeling;
Its touch absent as a shadow,
A scenic mystery exposed.
Like some Teutonic land fallow
From the sun's flash becomes deposed.

This black knight's net, a solid blot,
Cast as a huge blanket overall
Its temporary history—
A symbol vouchsafed, which cannot
Through recurrence once more fall
Until last to stay life's misery.

Dark pedigree, no known gender,
Drifts with fading density,
Contrasting the daylight blessing.
Such power this hidden sender
Captivates through great intensity—
An all-consuming recessing.

Driven back by artificial means
Human dimension defends life
With its ingenious return
To attack when deep shade clings.
But the dark work like a midwife
Crouches perennial concern.

The struggle against night's repose
Fought with the impatient day's speed
Toward the unknown is not greed.
For humans' desire to compose,
To extend the joust to succeed
More to yield the created seed.

Life's continuation to extend
Will ever test this valiant foe.
To fight the mist of unknown creed,
The battle will moreover fend.
No matter what light portends go,
It exalts time to live its deed.

Everyone Else

Passing over streets the many lights flickering
Under a black-and-gray sky headlights snickering.

As if they are horses lunging behind and around,
As if they cannot wait to claim the assuaged ground.

Rubber laps at the pavement shining from lights' beams,
Clawing and grabbing for more space as each one screams.

Hurrying, rushing to somewhere everyone else is;
Everyone compelled grappling an interlocking fizz.

Downhill the stream cuts through the pre-dawn light.
Farther away all seem to meld through the lost night.

A gold streak lines past devious intersections.
A determined trust craves to escape connections.

In front and behind the band grooves its lurid glare
Against the breaking day losing one's lull to stare.

Soon the middling trace will no longer have its draw
And then the dark will no longer express its awe.

Sensual Trespass

Thin whites and pale greens are left lying.
Looking, surveying, careful where to step
My vantage makes it all patchwork spying
As I sense there the waning moments crept.
Yesterday, white covered about three inches.
Today, searching moist-bent grass struggling
And each previous blade now wet flinches
To return its old vibrant self, struggling,
As blades do when compacted crystals remain;
The sun melts them to gradual flowing,
Ground water slipping into the soil drain.
As all of us want to straighten after,
Sloughing through downpour drenching rain,
Then the sun flares this dissolute rafter.
The snow, which once laid over weighted grass,
Only to soon lose its craven sea of white,
Now releases its sensual trespass.

Restoration

The leaves left mud-stuck by the rain
Cannot be drawn by wind sucked away.
Dried and then soapy wet those remain
Under scraggy trees, Winter's mainstay.

Arctic snows lost turn to less cold—
Nothing more than wetness to yet wait
Until the northern cloud drifts rolled
Across the massed sky slowly abate.

Bush branches shake in the piercing wind
Leafless in the root earth try survive
The push of mid-season air to bend-
And-not-break rushes to stay alive.

Bleakly exposed limbs suffer teased,
Then breezes come to blow less often.
After the cold torrents have eased,
Warm swishes start to come and soften.

Clouds separate and stall sunlit skies,
Sweeping half-hearted foggy days stray
Less thick to languish in swirling trics;
The shifting wet cold slowly creeps away.

Then appearing soon through bark roots
Little knobs bump out ready to insight
Waking to spurts of tiny stem shoots,
Startling evidence of a new leaf's might.

So opens nature's gaseous storage—
Countless reservoirs to supply growth
Brings the return miracle forage:
Plant and animal restoration of both.

Sunday Mind

Silent air brushes the floral leaf,
Leaving the cochlear canal free
To wait for any scant new brief
To pull the Sunday mind yet to see.
Quiet entreaty for the week's end,
Rests like a moat's claim to protect
Against a heart's felt need to defend
Latent prattle on what to expect.
Resounds the days' dubious torments.
Inner life mulching the wasted thoughts—
Buried insulation of remnants
Searching calm from perceived oughts.

The Star

More than a fleur-de-lis; more than a light flash;
No armorial bearing this glowing!
More like a golden attention strip sash
Stretching gently across in its flowing
Delicately, steadily toward a dwelling.
Who could tell in that crystalline night
But for this searching direction swelling
Onto the snow as it made such a sight.
Could one, would one gaze up with newborn eyes
And wonder, and be calmed by its greeting?
Three saw it as they came under its skies.
One night and forever all would be seeing.

Attitude

No more stately does the arbor vitae stand,
Unmoving in its posture stretching up
Tall and still returning even wind-blown
To its position planted there to stay.
Matching others in a row forms a fence
Of verdant freshness by a planting hand.
Once placed uprightly not as ground fillip
But an evergreen pyramid on its own
To grow and hold itself a noble way.
Erect it grows to be, to commence
In formation and without pretense.

Seamy Lift

Dreary gives way the day to the winded
Whitecaps, breeze rolling inflated water
Foams along in heaps and swells leaving
Almost as soon as they form on surface,
Once placid before air currents evolved;
Once clear and smooth invisible pressure
Releases the stretched invisible membrane
Like an empty capsule waiting, waiting.
Sun removed by cover of droopy clouds
Hanging between a used-to-be serene sky.
Pole flags waving against not quite fog
Being tried through its texture whipping.
Behind gray-silhouetted mountains lost
Until heat rays lift their stealthy wrap.
Seamy weather almost but not quite
Will presage a soon-to-be clarity.

A Mark

Glory comes in the sleeping bush
Renowned for its quiet submission.
Resistant to rain and wind's push,
It bends but returns without suspicion,
Standing and growing life has set
No mystery to its leafy stems
Stretching out and down a curving net,
Or even umbrella to the ground, skims
Clean on the shaded soil beneath.
Winter snows stick to its mounded shape,
Which it holds for weather's bequeath
Until the crystal melt ceases to drape
The cold and leave same as before,
But absorbs the moisture to live.
Beside a tree it rests to store
Like feet press a contour to give
Roots a cover should soil blow away.
Beside a building it gives a mark,
Otherwise a wall would bare display
A stiff foundation cold and stark.
To decorate a corner lot
Without any growth to give it style,
And round its pointy barren plot,
This bush could divide an aisle.
Dwarfed in size compared to a tree,
Yet it stands resolute to place
A mark, a curve so clear to see
And be where needs a striking face.

A Cross

Making a daily visit to the washing facilities
with nothing on my mind save that prismatic day,
as the light at the window sprinkled through the trees
adhering blotches refracted on the side of my house,
I readied myself for the release to come.
A blaze through the crinkled glass suddenly washed my face.
So strong was the radiated light that my eyes were drawn
though trying to withhold the pouring rays into my brain.
Reaching my hand up to stop the piercing constancy,
my outstretched fingers retracted together to bastion
the intensity at first glance of the blinding foray.
The breaking power of a cloud suffered for a moment.
Lowering my hand the glow became more concentrated
and the full blast contracted into a perfect symbol.
Slowly rising to my feet, trousers replaced, a figure
remained framed an immaculate blazing reality.
Unable to contain myself at its beauty enshrined,
finding the surety that emboldens believed senses
and hearing strange sighs unknowingly drifting from myself,
my loving wife came rushing to co-witness this creation.
Both stood amazed this delicate reflective light encased
A cross that day, never to be there for our witness again.

His Factor

Impacted is the eternal
Self-deepened further than time,
Then who knows the supernal
Does not skid, slow, or decline
Into nothingness with death.

Each day God offers repair
As sure as each day reappears.
Each day to climb His lofty stair
To live in opportunity, no fears
No matter if creeps despair.

Storms of life return and go
With lingering days adjust.
Who knows or is meant to know,
But the surface is only dust
One day comes the eternal flow.

Continues on life and after
Each way must be one's own
To climb above each rafter,
To wait each day's metronome.
To become one more, His factor.

Silent Ring

A whisper of pink leaves—out the cherry trees'
Alert, as early Spring divines to rue
The displacing lung of Winter's dying force,
That takes its leave aloof diminishing breezes.
Only hints of fresh fragrance alludes the true
Essence of nature's fomenter, the new course
Suggested by the delicate flowering growth.
Before had been the desolate limbs exposed,
When the autumnal season had begun its pale
Fall sweep's losing luster through vacant betroth,
That Winter's numbing blow overtakes disposed
To stifle young beauty launching its cold contrail.
The third season comes stealthily without friend,
Throwing forth its lengthening blank soul pause,
Distraught in its rush to maim life's renewal
With failing frigidity overwhelms to the end,
Which it hopes to induce detrimental flaws
To residing life subject to nature's approval.
But then, the flowering cherry will not go.
Coming back after Fall's loss of clothing, stands
In its signal beauty to reignite Spring.
This sight of return remarks in graceful flow.
Seen in contrast against the restrictive glands,
The colorful start blossoms through in silent ring.

Harbingers of Spring

My collapsed awning gives off creaks
In its folded retracted laps.
Could it be something in it speaks?
Something discovered in its traps,
Or little spaces wrinkled in it.
Little bleats told me take a peek
One soft morning in sunlit spray.
Early for Spring to show its face
When buds bulb up in new array.
Stepping out to see, peering wide
Above my paneled sliding door,
Tiny pieces of weed stems slide
Down on my head as I explore
To find two sparrows flying in.
The surest wake to Spring has come
Fluttering to build for a time when
Love's lure directs its notice from.

Unchanged

The dark in a cave remains that way
Until or unless some thrown spark
pierces the nervous tissue wash—
a process of variant ideas sway
former implantations so stark
as if they were lost in a marsh.

Islands of swamp water rest deep
drawn beyond the tall grass sunken
into a bayou offshoot filled
with drainage of muddy soil creep,
finding its settling place shrunken
to a long canal spring rain filled.

No access from the road made us
dislodge our skiff and wade the weeds,
carrying our wood boat down to it,
holding, with shoulders and arms truss.
We suffered the chin-high coarse beads
that scratched our necks trying to get
through to the water stung by sweat.

Soon a short mud shore left our rakes
of whelps to see a pea-green stream
where we lowered to slide the edge.
Then down to press the water snakes
wiggling their nest like a furied dream
forced a pause before slipped our wedge.

"Don't bother them, not bother you,"
one said. Leaving splashed behind
neither changed their minds as we paddled.
On we fished entering their slough,
their marsh, their cerebrum to find
within their world no change straddled.

Inspection

The duty roster had been placed
On the porch board tacked
down tightly as we faced
another week of uncertainty.

Floors were clean; bunks were made.
A short walk to the line remained
to start the day, make the grade
required to run the plane up.

Inside the hangar roll call
before walking with the tool box
across the ramp a day in Fall,
a little breezy the wind blew.

Clean coveralls, freshly shined boots
crossed the ramp in the latent sun.
Ours' on the end to pass the hoops
before our next inspection run.

Sitting erect on her landing gear,
four engine props all in line,
blades matching, waiting, no fear
to take all stresses to her design.

Walking proudly a job to do,
my young life moved eagerly,
tugs blowing by, passing through,
each to start the world machines.

Being a part of such power,
Such roaring well-timed beauty
built to cause others to cower
if they should test its strength.

Today, now a time long passed
no longer coveralled to achieve,
once a part of that measured cast,
time now has given a reprieve.

Once life simple to look into
now more time to pause and see
other measures age will construe.
New ways are caught for life to be.

Across the ramps, across runways,
something soars beyond what is seen.
So much thought for so many days
leaves little for what had been.

Glacial Touch

A morning clear sky few white cirrus
clouds across, parting for the mountain
left a view of a grand ice-cream mound.
Spread wide its glacial domain to fear us
reaching a trespass on its fountain,
frozen smooth high altitude half round,
was no concern for its magic presence.
Looking off and up gave wonder how far
we were to ride to have a closer view.
Standing and waiting to touch its essence,
would the wispy clouds fail to mar
our helicopter touching down anew
on the freshly frost-crusted crest.
Impatiently we paused, hoping soon
our flailing bird could clear to raise
us between the frivolous puffs to test
its sturdy skids like a balanced spoon
through the pristine cloud-topped maze.
We must fly when a hole appears.
Wind shifting vaporous masses
floated concealment for setting down.
Drawing enchantment disguises fears
and distance covers crevasses
as we yearned to reach the crown.
Then the watery vapors slid sideways,
so the sun glistened the frigid surface.
Quickly we rose and fluttered away,
lifting our lightened selves to stray,
overcoming the thermal preface
to climb the wintry cliff midday.
Wafting along over the tree line
to the peak, full view rose ahead
as we sat in the bubble cabin.
Sharply skimming arching this sign
of crystalline clarity read
a flat spot to settle safely in.

Now surrounded by an all-white
terrain, we felt a slight breaking crunch
that stilled our freedom-floating ride.
A searching moment craving sight
felt ourselves in a postured scrunch
as if we moved our craft would slide.
Assured we had stuck securely,
all were invited step out on the ice.
The permafrost held us to stand
still at first, then to stride demurely
to explore this level plain so precise
in its captivating purity grand
to both touch and sight there to be.
The clouds swiftly floated over us,
forcing to race back into our seats.
A miraculous tunnel we could see
formed leaving just enough retreat
to slip sideways down to the trees.
Glancing back we found sight no more.
Turning ahead to glide back replete,
sated with wonder of nature's degrees,
places remain on the earth to explore.

Water Transportation

Briefcase stowed and safety belt locked for an ordered start
To enter the day and find the way through a fractious
    downpour.
The roaring smacks on the roof made a cerebral test to depart
On a deafening journey through canyons of cars, feet on the
    floor
To be ready to brake or accelerate forward once more.
The vision was so dim to drive was to skim the surface water.
Slip starts and slide curves swooshed along on a deft dodging
    journey,
As the drops grew hyper for faster wipers, no faster starter
Seemed possible or probable lest it all became a tourney
For who would win the race, a faster pace to exceed a being.
Now Ford, on Buick, through traffic all with concentrated
    seeing.
So all went forward to find a location, reach a station
All over again, facing the elements through transportation.

The Same Path

A walk, some say, will make the break of day.
Or does the day make the walk a fresh way
To start the heart through the smells and eyesights
That ease the mind with breaths of life's delights.
But do not walk the same path each time out.
New thoughts can call some thoughts to think about
Not the same ol' places and the same ol' things,
Once seen holds one to no fresh mental flings
That new sights are apt to cause to alight
Upon the self for a grasp that one might
Take, be drawn to look, even search the unseen.
Sights never made may lend what things could mean.
A mind not drawn to search and find new things
Finds but a backward stance and what that brings.

A Driving Trip

Loaded seats and bulging trunk,
All are ready to go.
Morning lights inviting the road
To grope the trafficking flow.
Waves good-bye with matching feelings
Make leaving hard to do,
But new sights and breaking sounds
Cause moving, a journey through.
The many locales along the way
Take hoping hearts along.
The opening lanes to new cities
With parting local throng.
In each succeeding elevation,
Miles and miles escaping,
Only passing stays on our trek
With such voracious gaping
At all the persons where they live,
And go themselves away
Into the least crowded climes
Where they too will stay.
Night brings the creeping, prowling dark,
Which changes the driving mode,
And shrouds the intriguing sights,

And lengthens the load.
Concentrated too long compels a stop
To rest in a comforting place,
Where the faded night will not last
Then sun again on our faces.
Days passing by as do the towns
Settling behind as we pass.
Now become more flaccid in our seats

Over pavement as if were glass.
Up ahead come the climbing mountains.
A wooing drone is heard.
The landscape changes—more left alone,
And awe in every word.
Up and around the swinging curves,
Our car embraces still.
We wish for lanes to be wider.
Here found our traveling fill.
But soon the crest was found
For starting partly down,
Toward the valley sights below
To find another town.
The blowing sound of mountain breeze
Comes whistling through the grill.
Rocks give way to swaying trees,
So sights increase our thrill.
Along the many sloping draws
Affecting a steady speed,
Valleys come and go for the trip,
Directing an attending need.
Across the plains we often see,
Off in the distance,
A grazing animal in silhouette
For a slowing-down insistence.
Another town, another city we find
In days passing through.
Another lake or stream we find to bridge;
No wish instead we flew.
No matter where we went,
Sights were fresh to see.
It meant another time are we bent
For another trip to be.

Into a Christening

The glint of metal slid effortlessly through the amorphous fog.
A sheen appeared when the sun shone with glistening
Brightness on the riveted skin as if a climbing earth smog
In the endless space had been forced into a christening—
A purification of the stale air from a resulting disappearance.
Such direct light would leave no evident airy destruction.
Such brilliant reflection seemed to make a perfect clearance
Possible for an imagining gaze conceiving no filtering
    obstruction.
Life thereafter was so impossible for the viewer to comprehend!
What place beyond physical reality can a human actually see,
But by a magnificent detection that would he mentally defend;
Then by deduction must search for clarification of what could
    be?

Anxious Plights

Here is a world weakened with indecisions.
Longings exist for everyone to hide the truth;
But there are so many ingrained precisions,
So many anxious plights held under one roof—
Visions of what can be torn from what should be.
A want or surge to grasp, unable to clearly see
Blind qualities of sureness thought to be right.
Firm within is an innate character part
Preventing description, but a displayed fact
Made, and made conscious in a momentary act:
And then, afterward there strides a guilt-laden blight—
The truth from pain's residue wounds the heart,
And now no escape can the conscience detach
From that poorly made judgment, and resurrect
A new pure unsoiled life to merely attach
To the self a clean spirit, serene, correct.

Temporal Pull

Important that the clouds are vacant, dispersed
approvingly by the early sun stripping away the haze,
dependent on the backing of the azure flooding clear
soon, hopefully, with blazing light opening the atmosphere.

Now, shave, shower, dress, and search for what appeals
to the breakfast need, replenish energy to play the game—
thankful joy to enrich the heart and tantalize the mind—
visualize the flight of the ball and greens for the orb to find.

Catch the thrill shared by another's swing into a blue clear
sky, drying the moisture from the awakening grass;
or feel the power from sinewy strength to force the bend
of the shaft, flexing for a response for the sphere to ascend.

From their resting place retrieval of the metal sticks,
so prized for their precise weighted heads to strike
with a missilelike press, achieving straight drives—
sensations which kinesic first and then visual sense thrives.
Hope springs forth as all come ready to carve the journey
with the day showing its promise through rays of warmth,
beginning and seeking all who venture the fresh-cut grass
to display such temporal pull away into the trespass.

The Light

There transfixed, through a cold and supernal wind,
The light proclaiming came down where it would descend
To a place removed to find peace that would transcend.
Where found a place of animals close to warm their flanks.
An old place seemed different, where each felt their thanks.
There was a boxlike trough, though open, was filled—
Straw comforting frozen feet spread as if were spilled,
Though released on the ground under a weathered cover.
There is one corner protected by a few drowsy sheep,
Blocking a direct exposure for a night place to sleep,
Rested a husband and a mother nestling a baby just born.
There the light came through over the sheep unshorn,
From a bright star clearly seen traversing an open sky.
A trail well traveled to it could be taken for all to try—
Walked over so often human imprint kept it clear
To those who might come, witness, and have no fear.
That night on this trail was seen three approaching:
Three rode with gifts slowly so not to be encroaching.
All were coated by this one star, this revered light,
Reflecting the place so simply bathed in the pure light.
Would any who saw note the wonder of this instance?
Would any later feel the holiness of this remembrance?

Autumnal

The prelude to winter again has come.
To say again questions how old you are—
To make today such an autumnal plumb
Denotes my wonder how many so far,
Which asks for me how many more there are.

A Scavenger

The earth slips toward me in bulbous mass.
Some unknown geographies yet to be seen,
Though where I stand most of my time life will pass
Without having ventured to see the whole scene.
Its parts provide so much to know about life—
About moments lived in diverse cultures.
Once told stop trying to cut it with a knife—
Leave separating to ravenous vultures,
Who feed with no mind but to relieve hunger.
Is that what I have come to taste, all, everything,
When I go to feast myself like some monger,
Who wants to see only what to learn, a fling,
Hurling into places where life is just there;
Not here where I fail to think of life I see.
Must I travel distances to know, compare,
Or find here, where I am is a mystery?

Restricted View

Look back to see from the mirror image
The trailing concrete sliding back away
Into the sky larger than the city scape.
Like the mind grasp of key sights you manage,
From all you saw where you went the whole day,
And now cannot glimpse it in your escape.

The skyscape all melds into one big scene—
No more is any one-place story to be told.
Now the big picture seems an old fusion
Of clear and unclear breaks and edges between.
Large and small buildings since unseen, now bold
As if they grew in manacled protrusion.

But this is the world of art creation
With paint and brush to tie all together
In strokes to make one solid architecture.
Then one little glass, now a sensation
Has become fixed frame none can sever—
All the details held beyond departure.

Greater though is active mind than staid art,
Which must have against some space depicted.
Though all parts are touched in one stark view,
Yet an incident part can from the start
In the mind and heart be unrestricted—
Be, no matter surrounded, there anew.

Tube

By the wall stands a piece of steel and glass,
A place kept not yet moved from its spot.
On one side a plant, on the other a chair,
Just to give this block a guise for its mass.
Where else would it be to draw such a blot
On the room for soft talk with space to spare?
When its light is on in front, none may walk
To mar the view should such notice be made
Of what plot is shown or sought for a view.
Where did the desire go to enjoy talk,
And seek the time spent with someone to trade
What is known and dreamed living life through?
The time to share and learn from what is felt—
A friend or human being not bereft
Of what is learned from real contact drills—
Can best be found when speech readily fulfills.
A life to find through real discovery
May be the last hope for daily recovery.

Where Roads Are Worth More

Exciting journeys bring to mind airplanes or ships.
Preparations, itineraries, hotels remind us of trips.
We move ourselves to distant places for enticing days—
Some things new to see and people in different ways,
Though different only in cultures and degrees of freedom.
They walk odd streets but streets of their kingdom.
Pathways are not guarded, powers oversee their flow
Into larger areas where life will go and crowds grow.
Tourists go to feel and be somewhere else to be,
Smell different air, find different life architectures to see,
Witness things important from others' ways of life—
Life's conflicts taken for granted, with usual strife
Seeming so foreign to tourists who want to complain,
As they walk or ride with close poverty a daily refrain.

But who sees inside persons going to cluttered places,
Going to grasp wherewithal pushed into their faces,
Seeking eyes in tired directions with too many others,
Pursuing food for families, struggling fathers, worn mothers?
Their strides are long and their journeys are fixed;
The roads are crowded and their senses are mixed.

They must feel, but not too much beyond their own
Because time is limited and living space has not grown.
Go find from the land to pass over it from little yields.
Roads are worth more and space but barren fields.

Look inside there and find another important role;
Find there how to feel and stir from another soul.

Hidden Crest

Today became a very nice present—
The past lived are blurred moments grown
From energies wasted in time-torn lives.
Love was some particled incandescent,
Like a tide slipped by as a trailed unknown.

Sorrow leaves not psychic remembrance.
It holds but with a diminishing age
To be overcome, grotesque encumbrance,
A tedium that drags and drugs each new page.
Sweet caring sparingly mounts bereft age.

The sea rolls not with a glistening purity.
Staring from my bed, it waves with unrest—
As a mind filled with deepened insecurity.
A rented prow cuts through in powerful test.
What lies under surface flow, a hidden crest.

Life above or below must late contend,
Sometimes receive parts of heavenly rain
To disperse through what the sky will lend,
But there remains to be coursed with gain.
New hope arrives in satiating refrain.

Dear God, like the falling rain You come,
And touch the great sea mind with cleansing might,
Adding to or separating things from
The unhealthy thought, inhabiting plight
That strains inside and roves through waving sight.

In all its outward expanse stretching out,
We course through its vast crowded creation,
Amazing shaping as currents splay about;
Do not make us miss our destination
With sailing power and determination.

But continuous moisture You send down
The ongoing gift to squelch even the storm.
Through turbulent internals with a crown—
Waves changing, a disguised outer form;
Will ever there be a balancing norm?

Plundering Anticipation

Go see new places; anticipate their wonder.
Dream beyond your plans and speculate on the trip.
Install the mental ecstasy. Image plunder
From the unseen sights that the unknown will let slip
Into the conscious, breaking old sights asunder.

Envision new smells, new senses of terrains unfound.
Release the mind now cluttered with lingering needs
For silken spaces wherever to be distant found
To different exposures. Sow the searching seeds
Of longings to go away where curiosity feeds.

Is the world too big or transportation too small
To allow the seeker to attempt such reaches?
The pain of a troubled mind or spiritless fall
Must find surcease from all that daily life preaches.
The turmoil calm seems a virtuous pass for all.

Spikes of Blue

Standing deep in the lupine flowers and heather,
Hesitant, with groping eyes seeing the contrast
Between the tapering spikes of blue—breezy weather
Made me look around to see how the wind did blast
The natural growths together, wrenching so fast
The shrubby green and blue flowers in a blur.
Clumps of displaced color, syncopated, blown
By the air to a pulsating musical stir
That make me wonder the extent my mind had flown.

Below on this Canadian mountain my senses
Were taken for a brief tenseless splurge in real time.
Seeing this infinite number of trees, no fences
To hold majesty in, this place held me sublime.
It would not compare any my reason or rhyme
That had come with me there, no insidious crime
At all that I might attach or juxtapose then.
And here came the wind blow to heave across my feet,
Causing me to stumble myself down and look when
A rhythmic comparison made life's moment replete.

Big Sky

Such grace will not spill from any boundary—
Where it does start and where it does reside
Leaves the mind to muse about what foundry
May a founder somewhere let us decide.

But a mind holder may allow the turns,
Placing the eyes to look at all traces
Where its light tones may reflect how one learns
And grasps how small our lives in their places.

This big sky we can only connect to,
As we travel to look from locations
Great but little whatever we may construe.
Eyes secure no model specifications.

Road Travel

The early starts take the calm morning lights,
Fresh with the smell of grass sprinklers wet touch
On the surface of the cosmetic sights,
Slows down the rush to make time and miss much—
Miss the contrast of inside cool air
With the outside fragrance of mixed flowers.
Reload the trunk amid such parting flair
Of color and nostrils' sense of showers,
Coming later down the farm fields of grain;
Turning out onto macadam to leave,
The parkways made from artificial rain,
Going on for a day's ride to retrieve
Natural sights, roadside weeds where foxes hide.
Many birds fly up and wing the open sky,
Rushed by motored sounds or dangers beside.
Safe for them the sky waits when they must fly.
Trees thicken and peaks loom up to surprise.
They appear so soon and change the focus.
Higher pulls and bending roads hold the eyes.
Switchbacks force steering wheel change of locus,
Curving conditions coordinated
Over passes to a downhill mixed point
Must slow speeds to places originated.
Valleys spread where low roads conjoint.
Many miles slip on by large tranquil lakes,
Through thinning trees, towns in the distance.
Some small, meld into cities for brief meal breaks.
The evening approaches, claiming resistance.
The days have been long filled with searching.
Nights were avoided, for days held more to see.

Travel is always moving on, lurching,
Finding the old and the new, a mindful spree.
All roads lead back to where one started.
Coming back reflects from where one has departed.
How swift the travel through life's journeyed space.
Great land and water soothes the human race.

Between

The blue sky yet to come into view awaits contact.
Human hearts search mornings to find some semblance of day
For what instant will the proof peak and become a fact.
To seek the praise one must provide search time to defray
The cost of mental sharpness to pause just long enough,
Letting the life spirit hold in awaiting moments hence
When the mind and soul will not remove from cognate stuff;
An instant pause will fit the first moment to commence.
That time, that search must distill what essence life must be—
The joining and detaching of day from night there found.
No matter what words used to define what two can see,
The sense and meaning of speech comes from how we are
    bound.

Crater Lake

How proud my body was pulled in easy ascent toward!
My machine seemed amalgamed to ease me forward,
And today inclined under a clear blue canopy
Of sky that was open to rim the upcoming reward.
Higher yet my eyes wandered through the tree panoply—
Seemed so many as they did slope the hills with greenery.
They looked as if they were all attached in rolls
Of strength to bastion against what lay beneath.
So long ago active volcanos applied their tolls
When the earth was scorched but now made a wreath
To further clear the air and take the sun's bequeath.
The steady climb through those lovely masses
Did not belie the clearings yet to find,
Because what ancient earth distributed in ashes
Still rested on pumice plains seemingly so designed
That the open spaces rested there clean, unmaligned.
Up ahead and through pumice fields and tree lines,
People gathered from parked cars to broach the edges.
All wanted to stop and look down on distant times
Over the sides, rock mortared and railed, all did dredge
With their eyes up and down creased and coved wedges
Of stone left there as an effect of the volcanic strain,
Of a time long ago that still shows the earth king.
This crater now left to pocket the snow and rain,
Where inner gases were released once in a ferocious fling.

So now we gathered at this many-mile wide chasm,
Filled with the reflection of its cobalt blue water.
Will our scientific genius ever return such a spasm?
Will what we learned from long ago help us be smarter?

Come Back for Them

The rippling water seems to move faster in its flight.
The back sides of the flaps take on a push from the light,
Which creates a tide romp pressing into the rock beach.
As I watch, my senses want me to ignore this sight,
And look beyond the little flowing turmoil of each
To see a farther out view no longer what it was—
If indeed the small black slices of flippy water
Are not what they seem and my eyes are just playing tricks,
They cause me wonder why they draw me from the skyline.

The little details I see draw my eyes with slight flicks
As if the shutter on my camera by design
Detects all the movement to enlarge human focus.
But back I always point toward the racing ripples.
Such a bigger, striking scene is there in my locus,
Though these smaller number many in little tiny nipples,
Pushing up and onward as if the only water
Were they in their rush to go where erratic winds blow.

Some say why when they are detached from the scene.
Look up! Look out! Do not respect your eyes. Make them go
Toward the architectural line; see the picture clean.
But return I come to those innumerable flaps.
Each one must not be considered as disruptive.
They are water too, a part of the scene, noticed.
They are part of the sea, the least of which ensconced.

Return to Lost Being

Slip away on a journey to an old place—
An old place where not remembered before.
Leave behind friends, relatives, see new faces,
Looking back in the mind from a land's end shore,
Far as one can go without moving in too distant sea lanes
From settled places to see only gulls and tall wading cranes.
"Where will you go and when will you return?"
Questions usually asked in the short term
Are from when you were still there, some small concern.
But nothing from those unexpected, not firm
In the seeker's mind to soon forget once were you clearly
    known,
Now not even to grasp from daily progress you then have
    flown.
If one stares for awhile, wading cranes do move
And away in flight they go not seen there again.
Leaving that shallow spot where ebbed the smooth
Stilled water flows around it then did end.
Long term we forget those now, not even a mystery left
For those remaining dreamers to discuss who could be bereft.

Desire comes to go out from just one staid part.
The mind works to cognate some sole ancestor.
Search to be where one has never known to start,
A life discovered somewhere to sequester
That single something or someone in the universe of being,
A root, a connection, a monument to be known for seeing.

Elusion

Pregnant is not the chad of a stylus decision,
Nor is it other than the thrust of imprecision.

Though the mind may hiccup, make inference a response,
One's strength appears being devoid of being a dunce.

Heads are housings not formed there for conical caps—
They rest as places for positing clear thinking maps.

Answers to contests should not come from frequent guesses.
The breath of revealed actions comes when a thought blesses.

Those with the power to act must not escape the act,
To be is proven when power eludes not the fact.

Equine Mortality

Deterring faded white-washed planks with loose nails,
Around softened stride rendered sparse grass turf—
Sometimes looking out, sometimes brushing the rails,
Where hopeless space restricts the hoof-stridden earth.

Enclosed by somewhat superior beings, wait—
Wait should captor control open green grass freedom.
Stand still or stride through the enclosure's wide gate.
Closed allows him no release into their kingdom.

To venture from such a limited equine field
Into a broader world of multiple uteri
Must be weighed against some new expected yield,
Some new response beyond one's facility.

For interior species what may be discerned?
Now beauty, speed, and procreative nature,
Unless the meat and limb drive consumers turned,
Innumerable will place each creature.

But for a world where use is found to be worth,
And life is not considered for just mere self,
Where can caring real love of life be on earth?
Where may the limit be in the search for health?

The Deck

Removed but adjoined the rectangle extends—
Offset on a different level from others in the complex.
Use of it make sights to view outside trends,
Yet it must receive the wind and rain's battering effects.
Behind is a sliding glass door for artificial gains.
Sometimes the need comes to stand on its tile floor,
And grasp its piped rails to stretch from physical pains,
And let the nostrils take in mixtured air once more.
Like a platform from one's own apportioned abode
Above the street below to watch the traffic pass by,
Being aware there is this scion staring out at each mode,
Prevailing from such means one affords to travel by.
Such yearning comes to those who must work inside.
The sky above surrounding whatever constructed form;
The tops of trees, some high enough protrude to divide,
Depending what the season's naked blanchings may perform.
Flower arrangements from the trough hang from the rails.
A little of inside escapes to punctuate the view.
What will those inside push out in human details?
How will this appendage serve to classify anew?

Aspen Ovals

None seemed reluctant to rise in the air.
The trees hung on and left things as they were.
The puffing breeze swooped through the glare.
Lighter than air aspen ovals made my heart stir—
So sun brightened they seemed yellow,
Jumping and dancing on the whirling air.
That shining fall morning like a bellow
The air leaved my head and collared flair,
Causing me to reach with care to pick them off,
And turn my wide band of flannel back down—
Seemed a shame to hinder their rise aloft.
Their shimmering beauty came all around.
They had covered the little road with a layer,
Where we occasioned to step, stretch our legs,
And saunter through like any other city strayer.
Dark dirt edged road subject to strained drift
Matched the blackened weather-tasted trees,
All unabsolved on the back sides of a rift
I reasoned from past old shadowed decrees.
More breezes followed; more leaves found the dregs.
The sun made warm enough to stroll without a coat.
Looking down I became loath to step on them.
Up again they would come with unwritten note—
A caressed screen of gaiety there to trim
The road with a new spreading quilted float.

Living the Moment

The snow has come, the snow has gone.
The streets are clear, the traffic returns.
It's safe to drive through places unknown—
Landscapes anew, more trips one learns.

A book to leave for one more time—
A cozy place but life goes on.
Schedules are kept, choices are mine.
New friends to seek, new roles to hone.

Start the engine, listen for the sound.
It's there again. Press the pedal
And start to roll over the ground.
Something thrilling man and metal.

A miracle this gas machine—
Such easy work it gives to me!
Just turn the key. This land machine
Speeds me away like destiny.

Massive power my own behest!
Notwithstanding good things to come,
It gives a sense beyond the quest
To travel far, too, and then some.

Sometimes one feels keeping going—
Traverse the new on traveled roads,
Keep on beyond humdrum knowing;
Replace the old to new abodes.

But human beings like auto power
Soar on to temporary thrill;
Though each second, minute, or hour,
Can go so far and not fulfill.

One day my eyes caught this small boy,
As my auto horse strode the streets.
His little wheels were not his toy.
Each turn was not what he repeats
In his journey down the concrete blocks.
His trip was replete in the way;
Going was his seminal thought.
Each moment rode, to him, was all
That life did have and life had wrought.

The snow does come, the snow does go,
The rain does fall, the rivers flow.
We live our lives, God gives each day.
Wherever we go, we live the way.

Saguaro

Described as rearing their green-fluted columns,
Stalks scattered free like large branching candelabra,
This giant ranging cactus resists age, stands solemn
And tall, marking proud dignity and bravado,
Speaking from its impressive straight and grooved girth,
Proclaims, "I am saguaro of the Southwest desert."
Standing straight, circling, making beauty its worth,
The distant regions would appear vast and inert,
Miles of sand and sage dressed with other prickly forms
Of cactus on the far off hills and stretching plains
If not for these huge markers seen as desert norms—
Customary signs of attractive occupancy claims.

Interim Peace

Walking through the mountain heather in languid liturgy,
A narrow path crossed its way through to follow along.
The gurgling sound of running water seemed to lyre ahead
A search over a casual rise to see and feel a liquid song.
Such a massively bright sunlight day called for cooling shade.
My mind harbored a waterfall with a sanguine lake below.
Upon scanning this spacious plateau in its bell flowered glade,
The scent of liquid and flower fusion fed my nostrils,
And then, there it was, clear moisture in a catching pond.
Slightly descending I saw a shouldering tree beside;
The bark was smooth to the flat ground in such an open bond.
Between trim and touch an invitation seemed certain.
The path trodden down by others made like a glide
For me to sail as if by gentle breeze through a gauze curtain,
Drawn invisibly to allow me in without any stay
To be formally invited, a place of spalike rest,
To come away from human greed and felt tempests below.
Somehow never before had anything quelled my worldly test.
Enough room for a sit-down with my back a comforting fit;
Enough room for my legs to extend almost into the pool.
One last look into the heather and sky above to sit
On a warm beach, my body collapsed on this earthly stool.
It was mine for the moment of occupation and time.
My need was great, so closing my eyes if this were heaven,
If this were the way of feeling when all worries will cease
And tranquil minds will undergo or give self to calm sublime,
Then here on earth life can be found in safe interim peace.

Temporal Identities

The bare earth in damp wet climes moss appears
Around the feet of trees and planted rocks.
It grows and spreads itself over the ground
And lays its green cover, thriving in wetter years
As though it could clothe like a woman's smock,
To drape the colder flesh where nakedness is found.
Dense clusters make their prodigious surface display,
Extending over dampness, adding imprint of creeping age.
For it does slyly seem to take its length of notice
Without close scrutiny until it moves its porous way.
Were it not wild and slow to reach its thickened stage,
Swallowing cosmetic grass as if it were a poultice,
To heal as the emulsion to the bald stricken earth,
It would not be such an invading enemy to the landscaper,
Whereupon seeing such attachment to his horticulture
Must then apply his chemical death, creating a dearth
Of its spongy growth, restoring again a place safer—
A place his green blades can outgrow nature's venture.
Man and nature struggle for their temporal ways.
Each has its own means what controls to contrive.
Each must favor a disposition with its material claim.
Somewhere with time confusion invades the days
And there comes conflict in when and how to strive.
All relations fix on some identity to mean the same.
Beauty and value change as controls are applied.

A Rhythmic Peace

Under cover of banded skies
In starts a tide that draws my eyes.
It lures me pause; be still and stand,
And almost feel its reaching hand.
I watch to see the water ooze
Over the sand, up to my shoes.
Then drift away, away to lose
Until again, again to try
And hold my gaze to wonder why—
A surface sight such smooth release.
Somehow I think a rhythmic peace.
A rush, a swoosh, it makes a sound,
To call me look again straight down.
I cannot help but see it move
To wash a place and swirl a groove
Into the moist and softened reach
It takes to clean the porous beach.
Out, out it flows. I cannot tell
How far it will to fill a swell,
And pull again in larger toll
And lose itself in greater roll.
Sometimes I think to take the bait;
(I'll leave my shoes, no longer wait
And join in this tumultuous throw.)
But then strange wind begins to blow.
My heart will not retreat the tow
To hold myself to other drives—
To continue with other lives;
Lest I return to feel the sea
If but to guess it means to me.